Google Pixel 9 Pro Complete Guide to Mastering AI-Powered Features and Android 15

Unlock Expert Tips for Setup Customization Camera AI Tools and Troubleshooting

Elara Technova

COPYRIGHT

✷ Elara Technova

Disclaimer

This guide is an independent publication and is not affiliated with or endorsed by the manufacturer of the product. All trademarks and product names are the property of their respective owners. While every effort has been made to ensure accuracy, the author and publisher are not liable for any errors, omissions, or outcomes resulting from the use of this guide. For official support, refer to the product manufacturer.

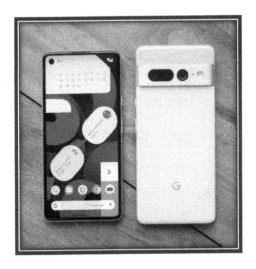

❋ *Elara Technova*

About the Author

Elara Technova is a trusted authority in technology writing, known for her remarkable ability to make complex concepts clear and approachable. With a strong background in Computer Science, she masterfully transforms intricate technical details into practical, step-by-step guides. Her work empowers readers of all skill levels to confidently understand and use the latest technology, making it accessible for everyone in today's rapidly advancing digital world.

✳ Elara Technova

Contents

Introduction

The Google Pixel 9 Pro represents the latest innovation in Google's flagship smartphone lineup, combining cutting-edge hardware with advanced artificial intelligence to deliver a seamless and intuitive user experience. As part of Google's continuous evolution in smartphone technology, this device pushes the boundaries of what users can expect from a modern smartphone, offering top-tier performance, an enhanced camera system, and a host of AI-driven features designed to simplify everyday tasks. This guide will help users unlock the full potential of their Pixel 9 Pro, covering everything from setup and customization to advanced photography and troubleshooting.

The Evolution of Google Pixel Phones

Google's Pixel lineup has consistently been at the forefront of Android innovation, pioneering features that have influenced the entire smartphone industry. The first Pixel device, launched in 2016, set the standard for AI-driven photography with its computational photography features, proving that great smartphone cameras are about more than just megapixels. Over the years, Google has refined its devices, introducing features such as Night Sight for low-light photography, Super Res Zoom for enhanced clarity, and real-time speech recognition powered by on-device AI.

The Pixel 9 Pro continues this legacy, building upon the advancements of previous models such as the Pixel 7 Pro and Pixel 8 Pro. With the introduction of the Tensor G4 chip, Google has taken AI integration to the next level, improving everything from battery optimization to real-time language translation. The camera system has also seen significant upgrades, making the Pixel 9 Pro one of the best choices for mobile photography enthusiasts. This evolution reflects Google's commitment to pushing smartphone capabilities forward, ensuring that users get a device that not only meets their current needs but is also future-proofed for emerging technologies.

The Google Pixel 9 Pro is designed to provide an unparalleled smartphone experience, combining high-end hardware with software that is optimized for efficiency and ease of use. One of its most notable features is the Tensor G4 processor, which enhances performance across various applications, particularly in AI and machine learning tasks. This ensures that features like speech-to-text, real-time translation, and photo processing are faster and more accurate than ever before.

The camera system remains a major highlight, with a triple-lens setup that includes an upgraded 50MP main sensor, an ultra-wide lens, and an improved periscope telephoto lens for superior zoom capabilities. Thanks to advanced AI-driven software, the Pixel 9 Pro can capture incredibly detailed images even in challenging lighting conditions, making it a powerful tool for both casual users and professional photographers.

Another significant upgrade is the 120Hz OLED display, which offers ultra-smooth scrolling and vibrant colors, enhancing everything from web browsing to gaming. The battery life has also been optimized through AI-powered adaptive battery technology, ensuring that the phone lasts longer on a single charge while maintaining peak performance.

Security is another area where the Pixel 9 Pro excels, featuring Google's Titan M3 security chip, Face Unlock, Fingerprint Scanner, and built-in VPN support for enhanced privacy. Additionally, Google's commitment to software updates means that users will continue to receive regular security patches and new features, keeping their devices up-to-date for years to come.

Why This Guide is Essential for Users

While the Google Pixel 9 Pro is packed with powerful features, many users may not be aware of how to take full advantage of them. This guide is designed to bridge that gap by offering step-by-step instructions on everything from basic setup to advanced customization and troubleshooting. Whether you are a first-time Pixel user or upgrading from a previous model, this guide will help you navigate the device's features efficiently.

For photography enthusiasts, this guide provides insights into AI-powered photography, manual camera settings, and how to get the best shots in different lighting conditions. If you are a business professional, you will learn how to optimize the Pixel 9 Pro for productivity, including managing emails, video conferencing, and using cloud storage effectively. Gamers will benefit from tips on optimizing performance for high-end gaming, while content creators can explore video editing, social media integration, and AI-enhanced creative tools.

Additionally, this guide includes a troubleshooting section, covering common problems such as connectivity issues, app crashes, and battery drainage, along with practical solutions to keep your device running smoothly. It also explores hidden features and shortcuts that can enhance your overall experience, ensuring that you are making the most of your Pixel 9 Pro.

Unboxing and First Impressions

When you first receive your Google Pixel 9 Pro, the unboxing experience is designed to be both premium and environmentally friendly. Google has continued its commitment to sustainability by using minimalist packaging made from recycled materials, while still ensuring that users get a well-protected device.

Inside the box, you will find:

- Google Pixel 9 Pro smartphone
- USB-C to USB-C cable (for fast charging and data transfer)
- Quick Switch Adapter (for transferring data from an old phone)
- SIM ejector tool
- Quick start guide and safety information

Upon holding the Pixel 9 Pro for the first time, the premium build quality is immediately noticeable. The device features a sleek aluminum frame, curved edges, and Gorilla Glass protection on both the front and back.

Despite its large display, it remains comfortable to hold, thanks to its ergonomic design. The buttons are well-placed for easy accessibility, and the haptic feedback feels refined and responsive.

The display is another standout feature, with its vibrant OLED screen offering deep blacks, high brightness levels, and smooth 120Hz refresh rate, making scrolling and animations fluid. The always-on display allows you to check notifications, date, and time at a glance without waking up the device.

The setup process is straightforward, with on-screen prompts guiding users through the initial configuration. During setup, you will be asked to sign in with your Google account, restore data from a previous device, and customize preferences such as display settings, Google Assistant, and security options. The Quick Switch Adapter makes data transfer seamless, ensuring that contacts, apps, and settings from your old phone are easily carried over.

Once the setup is complete, the Pixel 9 Pro's home screen presents a clean and intuitive interface, featuring Google's Material You design, which automatically adapts the color theme based on your wallpaper. Pre-installed Google apps such as Gmail, Google Maps, Google Photos, and YouTube are neatly organized, ready to be used.

From the moment you start using the Google Pixel 9 Pro, it is evident that this device is designed to offer speed, intelligence, and ease of use. Whether you are drawn to its AI-powered features, pro-grade camera system, or seamless integration with Google services, this phone is built to handle everything from daily productivity to high-performance tasks with ease.

❋ Elara Technova

Setting Up Your Google Pixel 9 Pro

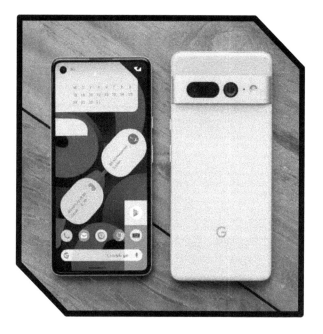

S etting up your Google Pixel 9 Pro properly ensures a smooth and personalized user experience. Whether you are upgrading from an older Pixel device or switching from another smartphone brand, the initial setup process is designed to be straightforward and intuitive. Google has optimized the onboarding experience to be fast, efficient, and user-friendly, allowing you to configure essential settings, transfer important data, and personalize the device to suit your needs.

This chapter will provide a step-by-step guide on setting up your Pixel 9 Pro, including powering on the device, selecting language preferences, connecting to the internet, signing into your Google account, and transferring data from your previous device. Proper setup ensures that all features, including Google Assistant, cloud backups, and security settings, are configured correctly, giving you the best possible experience.

Getting Started with the Initial Setup

When you first unbox your Google Pixel 9 Pro, ensure that the device has sufficient battery charge before starting the setup process. If the battery level is low, connect the phone to a power source using the USB-C cable and charger included in the box. The Pixel 9 Pro supports fast charging, so you won't have to wait long before proceeding with the setup.

To turn on the device, press and hold the power button on the right side of the phone until the Google logo appears on the screen. Once powered on, you will be prompted to select your preferred language. This is the language that will be used for system navigation, menus, and voice commands. You can always change this setting later under System Preferences.

Next, you will be guided through connecting to a Wi-Fi network or inserting a SIM card if you are using mobile data. A stable internet connection is required for the setup process to proceed smoothly. If your device is carrier-locked, make sure you have activated your SIM card before inserting it into the SIM tray using the SIM ejector tool provided in the box.

After establishing a connection, you will be prompted to sign in with your Google account. This step is crucial as it syncs your contacts, emails, Google Photos, Drive, Play Store apps, and other personalized settings from your previous device. If you don't have a Google account, you can create one during setup.

You will also be asked to set up Google services, such as Google Assistant, location access, automatic backups, and device security features. These settings enhance your phone's functionality, allowing seamless access to Google's ecosystem. You can choose to enable or disable each service based on your preferences.

Transferring Data from Your Old Device

One of the most critical steps in setting up your Google Pixel 9 Pro is transferring data from your previous smartphone. Google makes this process incredibly easy, offering multiple ways to migrate your important files, contacts, and apps.

If you are switching from an older Pixel or Android device, the Quick Switch Adapter (USB-C to USB-A adapter) included in the box allows for fast, direct data transfer. Simply connect both devices using a USB cable and follow the on-screen instructions to move your contacts, call logs, text messages, photos, videos, and apps to your new Pixel 9 Pro.

For those switching from an iPhone, Google offers a dedicated "Switch to Android" app available in the Apple App Store. This tool transfers contacts, photos, videos, and even iCloud data to your Google account. Additionally, you can sync your Google Photos and Google Drive to ensure that your files are backed up and accessible on your new device.

If you prefer a wireless transfer, the Google Pixel 9 Pro supports data migration via Wi-Fi. During setup, you can select "Restore from a Backup", which allows you to retrieve apps, settings, and files from your Google Drive backup. This is a convenient option for users who have backed up their previous device to the cloud.

After transferring data, it's important to verify that all essential files and apps have successfully migrated. Check your contacts, photos, and messages to ensure nothing is missing. If necessary, you can manually reinstall apps from the Google Play Store and log back into accounts that may require authentication.

Connecting to Wi-Fi and Cellular Networks

To fully utilize the capabilities of the Google Pixel 9 Pro, you need to establish a reliable internet connection.

The device supports Wi-Fi 6E, ensuring fast and stable connections, and is also compatible with 5G networks for high-speed mobile data.

To connect to Wi-Fi, navigate to Settings > Network & Internet > Wi-Fi and select your preferred network. If the network is password-protected, enter the credentials and confirm the connection. Wi-Fi is recommended for downloading updates, restoring backups, and installing essential apps during setup.

If you are using mobile data, ensure that your SIM card is properly inserted. The Pixel 9 Pro supports both physical SIM and eSIM, allowing flexibility in how you activate your cellular plan. If your carrier supports eSIM, you can activate your number by scanning a QR code provided by your mobile service provider.

For those traveling internationally, Dual SIM Dual Standby (DSDS) functionality allows you to use two numbers simultaneously, making it easy to switch between carriers. To configure your mobile network settings, go to Settings > Network & Internet > SIMs and select the appropriate options for your data plan.

If you experience issues connecting to a network, ensure that airplane mode is turned off, and restart your device if necessary. Additionally, verify that your APN (Access Point Name) settings are correctly configured, as some carriers require manual input for mobile data access.

Google Account Integration and Syncing

Your Google account is the key to unlocking the full potential of the Pixel 9 Pro, enabling seamless synchronization across all Google services. Upon signing in during setup, the device automatically syncs emails, contacts, calendar events, Google Photos, Google Drive, and app data, ensuring a smooth transition from your previous device.

For users who rely on Google Assistant, enabling voice commands allows hands-free operation, from setting reminders to controlling smart home devices. Navigate to Settings > Google > Google Assistant to customize voice recognition, personal results, and routines for a more tailored experience.

To optimize Google Photos backup, go to Settings > Google > Backup & Sync, where you can select upload quality options and ensure that your photos are safely stored in the cloud. Google offers unlimited storage for compressed photos, while full-resolution images count towards your Google Drive quota.

For added security, you can enable two-step verification for your Google account. This provides an extra layer of protection, ensuring that unauthorized users cannot access your data. Additionally, reviewing your Google Account privacy settings allows you to control what information is shared with apps and services.

If you use multiple Google accounts, the Pixel 9 Pro supports multiple user profiles, allowing you to switch between different accounts effortlessly. This is useful for separating work and personal data or managing multiple Google services efficiently.

By integrating your Google account during setup, you ensure that all essential services, including Google Drive, Google Docs, Google Meet, and Google Maps, function seamlessly across devices. The Pixel 9 Pro is designed to work within Google's ecosystem, making account synchronization a crucial part of the setup process.

Setting up your Google Pixel 9 Pro correctly is essential for a smooth and efficient user experience. From transferring data and connecting to networks to configuring Google services, each step plays a crucial role in optimizing your device. The next chapter will explore customization options, home screen personalization, and optimizing the user interface for better efficiency, ensuring that your Pixel 9 Pro is tailored to your preferences.

❋ Elara Technova

Exploring the Tensor G4 Chip

The Google Pixel 9 Pro is powered by the Tensor G4 chip, a significant upgrade from its predecessor, designed to enhance performance, improve battery efficiency, and introduce new artificial intelligence (AI) capabilities. Google's Tensor chip series is built to optimize machine learning and real-time computing, ensuring that the Pixel 9 Pro operates smoothly while delivering advanced features such as faster image processing, real-time language translation, and improved security measures.

The Tensor G4 chip plays a crucial role in improving the overall speed and responsiveness of the Pixel 9 Pro. Unlike traditional processors that primarily focus on raw computing power, Tensor G4 is designed to enhance AI-driven tasks, ensuring that Google's smart features, such as Google Assistant, on-device dictation, and advanced computational photography, function seamlessly. This chapter explores the performance improvements, battery optimizations, real-world application, and security enhancements of the Tensor G4 chip, giving you a deep understanding of how this processor makes the Pixel 9 Pro more powerful and efficient than ever.

Performance Upgrades and AI Enhancements

One of the most notable upgrades with the Tensor G4 chip is its AI-driven performance enhancements. Google has fine-tuned this processor to ensure that the Pixel 9 Pro operates faster, with smoother app transitions, quicker response times, and enhanced AI-powered automation. With a more efficient CPU and GPU architecture, the Tensor G4 chip boosts app launch speeds, gaming performance, and real-time image processing, making everyday tasks feel effortless.

The AI-powered enhancements allow the device to intelligently adapt to user behavior, improving the overall user experience. For example, the Pixel 9 Pro can anticipate which apps you frequently use and keep them active in the background while minimizing power consumption for less-used applications. This results in faster multitasking and a more seamless user experience.

Another remarkable AI-driven feature is real-time speech recognition and on-device translation. With the Tensor G4 chip, Google Assistant is faster and more responsive, enabling instant voice commands and real-time transcription without requiring an internet connection. The improved Live Translate feature allows for smooth, real-time conversations across multiple languages, making communication more accessible and intuitive.

Additionally, photo and video processing capabilities have been significantly improved. The Google Pixel 9 Pro's camera system relies heavily on AI enhancements, allowing for instant image processing, improved night photography, and real-time HDR rendering. Whether you're taking high-resolution photos or recording 4K videos, the Tensor G4 ensures that images are processed quickly and efficiently, delivering exceptional detail and clarity.

How the Tensor G4 Optimizes Battery Life

A key area of improvement in the Tensor G4 chip is its power efficiency. While raw performance is important, Google has designed this processor to optimize battery life, ensuring that users can enjoy longer usage without frequent charging.

The Tensor G4 integrates adaptive battery management, which learns user habits and allocates power intelligently. If you frequently use certain apps, the chip prioritizes battery usage for those apps while limiting background activity for less-used applications. This helps reduce unnecessary battery drain, extending the device's lifespan throughout the day.

Google has also improved the efficiency of background processing, ensuring that power is not wasted on apps running in the background. For example, if an app is consuming too much energy while idle, Tensor G4 automatically limits its resource usage, preventing unnecessary power drain.

The Pixel 9 Pro also benefits from enhanced cooling efficiency. The Tensor G4 chip is designed to run cooler under heavy workloads, preventing overheating while ensuring that the device maintains consistent performance over extended periods. This means that whether you're gaming, streaming, or multitasking, the phone remains responsive without rapidly depleting battery life.

Another notable feature is the improved adaptive refresh rate. The Pixel 9 Pro's display intelligently adjusts its refresh rate based on the content being viewed, reducing power consumption when high refresh rates are unnecessary. Combined with Tensor G4's efficiency-focused design, this results in longer screen-on time and a more power-efficient display experience.

Real-World Performance in Gaming and Multitasking

The Tensor G4 chip significantly enhances gaming and multitasking performance, ensuring that the Pixel 9 Pro remains competitive with flagship devices from other manufacturers.

For gamers, the improved GPU architecture delivers smoother frame rates, faster load times, and more detailed graphics rendering. The Tensor G4 enables hardware-accelerated ray tracing, allowing for better lighting effects, reflections, and shadows in supported games. Whether you are playing graphics-intensive games like Genshin Impact, Call of Duty Mobile, or Asphalt 9, the Tensor G4 ensures a seamless and immersive experience.

Another key improvement is heat management. Many flagship smartphones experience performance throttling during prolonged gaming sessions, but Tensor G4's efficient power distribution ensures that the Pixel 9 Pro can maintain high performance without excessive heat buildup. This results in more consistent gameplay without frame rate drops.

For multitasking, the Pixel 9 Pro benefits from Tensor G4's AI-powered app optimization. You can run multiple applications simultaneously, switch between apps effortlessly, and use features like split-screen mode or picture-in-picture without lag. Google's RAM management has also been improved, ensuring that background apps remain active without consuming excessive resources.

Security Features Powered by the Tensor G4

Security is a major focus for Google, and the Tensor G4 chip brings substantial improvements in device protection and data security. The Pixel 9 Pro is one of the most secure Android devices, featuring advanced security layers powered by Tensor's AI-driven security measures.

One of the most significant upgrades is the Titan M2 security chip, which works alongside the Tensor G4 to protect sensitive data, encrypt passwords, and safeguard against malware attacks. The Pixel 9 Pro benefits from end-to-end security, ensuring that biometric authentication, payments, and personal data remain secure from potential threats.

The Google Pixel 9 Pro also includes an improved anti-phishing and anti-malware system, powered by AI. The Tensor G4 automatically scans for suspicious links, apps, and downloads, warning users of potential security risks. Additionally, on-device threat detection prevents unauthorized access by monitoring app behavior and alerting users if an app engages in suspicious activity.

Another security enhancement is real-time facial and fingerprint recognition improvements. Tensor G4 optimizes Face Unlock and the under-display fingerprint scanner, ensuring faster and more accurate authentication while enhancing fraud detection.

The Pixel 9 Pro also benefits from Google's AI-powered security updates. Instead of waiting for full system updates, Tensor G4 enables seamless security patches that are delivered in the background, ensuring that your device remains protected against vulnerabilities at all times.

In addition, Google provides seven years of software and security updates, meaning the Pixel 9 Pro will receive long-term support, ensuring it remains secure and up to date for years to come.

The Tensor G4 chip is the heart of the Google Pixel 9 Pro, delivering cutting-edge performance, enhanced AI capabilities, and unparalleled security measures. From faster processing speeds and improved gaming performance to extended battery life and top-tier security enhancements, this processor ensures that the Pixel 9 Pro remains a powerhouse in the smartphone industry.

Display and Design Optimization

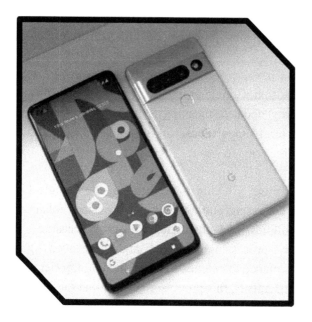

The Google Pixel 9 Pro introduces a stunning 120Hz OLED display that enhances the user experience with vibrant colors, smooth motion, and optimized brightness levels. Google has crafted this high-resolution panel to offer a visually immersive experience, whether you are watching videos, gaming, or simply browsing the web. This chapter explores the advanced display features, adaptive brightness controls, customization options, and ways to protect the screen from damage. Understanding these elements will help users get the most out of their Pixel 9 Pro's display while ensuring longevity and optimal usability.

Ultra-Smooth 120Hz OLED Display Features

One of the standout features of the Google Pixel 9 Pro is its 6.7-inch OLED display with a 120Hz refresh rate. This ensures that scrolling, animations, and transitions feel buttery smooth and responsive. The high refresh rate makes a noticeable difference when navigating menus, playing fast-paced games, or even reading text, as the movement on the screen appears fluid and effortless.

The OLED panel offers exceptional color accuracy, deep blacks, and high contrast levels, making everything from photos to videos appear crisp and lifelike. Compared to LCD screens, OLED technology provides individually lit pixels, which allows for better energy efficiency and true black levels. This means that when the screen displays dark themes or black backgrounds, those pixels remain off, saving battery life.

Google has also optimized the Pixel 9 Pro's display for HDR10+ content, allowing users to enjoy vibrant colors and enhanced dynamic range when watching videos on streaming platforms like Netflix, YouTube, and Amazon Prime Video. The higher brightness levels ensure excellent outdoor visibility, even under direct sunlight, making it easier to read messages, browse the web, or take photos without struggling with glare.

Additionally, Google's adaptive refresh rate technology ensures that the Pixel 9 Pro dynamically switches between 1Hz and 120Hz depending on the task at hand. If you are scrolling or playing a game, the screen automatically operates at 120Hz for smooth responsiveness, but if you are reading a static page or viewing an image, it reduces the refresh rate to 1Hz to conserve battery life. This intelligent power management system allows users to enjoy the benefits of a high-refresh-rate display without sacrificing battery efficiency.

Adaptive Brightness and Color Customization

Google has refined the adaptive brightness system in the Pixel 9 Pro, ensuring that the screen adjusts automatically based on surrounding lighting conditions. The device uses AI-powered sensors to analyze ambient light levels and user preferences over time, gradually learning your habits to provide an optimal brightness setting for every situation.

For instance, if you frequently adjust the brightness while using the device in a dimly lit room, the Pixel 9 Pro's AI system will remember this preference and automatically lower the brightness when similar conditions arise. This eliminates the need for manual adjustments and ensures that the display remains comfortable on the eyes in various lighting environments.

In addition to brightness optimization, the Pixel 9 Pro offers advanced color customization options. Users can fine-tune the color profile of the display by choosing between:

- Natural Mode – Provides true-to-life colors with accurate color reproduction.
- Boosted Mode – Enhances color vibrancy while maintaining a balanced, realistic look.
- Adaptive Mode – Uses AI to automatically adjust colors based on on-screen content.

For those who prefer warmer or cooler tones, the Pixel 9 Pro includes manual color temperature adjustments, allowing users to fine-tune the display's warmth or coolness to suit their preferences. This is particularly useful for individuals who spend long hours reading or working on their devices, as warmer tones can reduce eye strain.

Always-On Display: Uses and Customization

The Always-On Display (AOD) is a convenient feature of the Pixel 9 Pro, allowing users to view key information such as time, date, notifications, and battery percentage without waking the screen. This feature leverages OLED technology, ensuring that only the necessary pixels remain lit while the rest of the screen remains off, conserving battery life while providing essential updates at a glance.

Google has enhanced the customization options for the Always-On Display, allowing users to:

- Choose clock styles – Select from various digital and analog clock designs.
- Show or hide notifications – Customize which notifications appear on the Always-On Display.
- Enable music recognition – The Now Playing feature automatically identifies songs playing in the background and displays the track title on the AOD.
- Battery percentage display – Users can opt to keep battery status visible even when the screen is off.

One of the most impressive additions is At a Glance, a Google AI-powered feature that provides real-time information based on location, calendar events, and weather updates. This means users can view upcoming appointments, traffic conditions, or package delivery updates right from their Always-On Display without unlocking their phone.

For users concerned about burn-in issues, Google has implemented pixel shifting technology, which subtly moves static elements around the screen over time to prevent image retention. This ensures that long-term use of the Always-On Display does not cause permanent screen damage.

Protecting the Pixel 9 Pro's display is essential to maintain clarity, responsiveness, and durability. Even though Google uses Corning Gorilla Glass Victus for enhanced scratch resistance, the screen is still vulnerable to accidental drops, smudges, and fingerprints. Investing in a high-quality screen protector and case ensures that the device remains in pristine condition for years to come.

There are two main types of screen protectors to consider:

- Tempered Glass Protectors – These offer the best protection against scratches, drops, and impact damage. They provide a smooth, glass-like feel, maintaining the original touch sensitivity and clarity of the display.
- Matte/Anti-Glare Screen Protectors – Ideal for users who frequently work outdoors, as they reduce reflections and fingerprint smudges while maintaining a smooth touch experience.

For cases, users should consider:

- Rugged Cases – These provide maximum drop protection, making them ideal for individuals who frequently travel or work in rough environments.

- Slim and Transparent Cases – Designed for those who prefer lightweight protection without compromising the phone's sleek design.
- Wallet Cases – These include cardholders and foldable covers, offering added convenience for users who want to carry essentials without a separate wallet.

Additionally, screen protectors with oleophobic coatings help reduce fingerprints and smudges, ensuring that the screen remains clear and easy to clean. When paired with a durable case, users can significantly reduce the risk of display damage while maintaining the premium look and feel of the Pixel 9 Pro.

The Google Pixel 9 Pro's 120Hz OLED display delivers an exceptional visual experience, combining fluid motion, accurate color reproduction, and advanced customization features. Whether you're a casual user, mobile gamer, or professional content creator, optimizing the display settings can significantly enhance usability and comfort.

✳ Elara Technova

Mastering the Android 15 Operating System

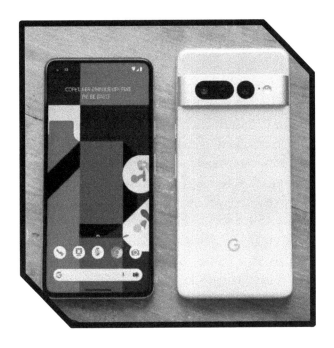

The Google Pixel 9 Pro runs on Android 15, the latest iteration of Google's powerful mobile operating system. With enhanced security, smoother navigation, improved customization options, and better efficiency, Android 15 refines the overall Pixel experience by introducing new AI-driven features, system optimizations, and enhanced multitasking tools.

Understanding how to navigate and customize Android 15 is essential to maximizing the potential of your Pixel 9 Pro. This chapter covers everything you need to know about the new updates, user interface enhancements, and hidden features that make your smartphone experience smoother and more personalized.

What's New in Android 15 for Pixel 9 Pro

Android 15 brings several key improvements, making the Pixel 9 Pro more powerful, intuitive, and efficient. One of the standout upgrades is the enhanced battery optimization system, which uses AI to predict which apps you frequently use and which ones can be put into deep sleep mode to preserve battery life. This results in longer screen-on times and improved background app management, ensuring that your device remains responsive without excessive power consumption.

Another major improvement is the Adaptive Touch Sensitivity feature, which adjusts screen responsiveness based on user interaction, environmental conditions, and accessories such as screen protectors or gloves. This ensures seamless usability in all conditions, making interactions with the Pixel 9 Pro's 120Hz OLED display even more fluid and precise.

Android 15 also enhances app launch speeds and system-wide performance. Google has introduced memory efficiency upgrades, meaning apps open faster, transitions feel smoother, and background tasks are handled more intelligently. For users who rely on multitasking, these optimizations create a lag-free experience when switching between applications or working on multiple tasks simultaneously.

Another exciting addition is AI-generated Smart Replies and Predictive Actions. These features use machine learning to suggest responses, actions, or shortcuts based on your conversations and app usage patterns. Whether you're responding to a text, sharing a file, or opening frequently used apps, Android 15 learns your habits and recommends relevant actions to save time and effort.

Navigating the User Interface

The user interface (UI) of Android 15 on the Pixel 9 Pro has been designed to be more intuitive and visually appealing. The home screen layout remains clean and customizable, while the gesture-based navigation system ensures quick access to apps and system features.

One of the most useful aspects of the Android 15 UI is fluid gesture navigation. Instead of relying on traditional navigation buttons, users can swipe up to go home, swipe from the edges to go back, and swipe up and hold to access recent apps. This system makes the user experience smoother and faster, particularly on the Pixel 9 Pro's high-refresh-rate display.

Google has also improved the notification center and quick settings panel, making them more accessible and functional. The new notification management system allows users to prioritize important notifications, group similar alerts, and dismiss unnecessary ones with a single swipe. Additionally, media playback controls are now integrated into the quick settings panel, making it easier to manage music, podcasts, or videos without opening individual apps.

For users who prefer customization, Android 15 offers more control over icons, themes, and wallpapers. With the Material You design system, users can apply dynamic colors that match the wallpaper, system accents, and app interfaces, creating a cohesive and personalized look across the entire device.

Customizing Widgets and Quick Settings

Widgets play an essential role in enhancing the functionality of the Pixel 9 Pro, allowing users to access information quickly without opening full applications. With Android 15, widgets have been redesigned to be more interactive and useful, providing real-time updates, expanded customization options, and improved adaptability.

Some of the best widgets available on the Pixel 9 Pro include:

- At a Glance Widget – Displays important details such as weather, calendar events, traffic updates, and flight schedules, all in one place.
- Google Calendar Widget – Allows users to view upcoming appointments, set reminders, and manage their schedules efficiently.

- Battery and Device Care Widget – Provides real-time battery percentage and device optimization recommendations.
- Google Assistant Snapshot Widget – Offers AI-powered recommendations based on your daily activities, such as reminders, news updates, and commute suggestions.

Additionally, the Quick Settings panel in Android 15 has been redesigned to make important toggles more accessible and functional. Users can now customize the Quick Settings menu by adding frequently used features such as Wi-Fi, Bluetooth, Dark Mode, Battery Saver, and Focus Mode, ensuring they have quick access to essential functions without digging through menus.

For users who rely on voice commands, Google Assistant has been deeply integrated into the Quick Settings panel, allowing for faster execution of voice commands without needing to unlock the phone. Whether you want to control smart home devices, send a message, or check your daily agenda, Google Assistant is now more responsive and context-aware than ever before.

Best Hidden Features in Android 15

Android 15 introduces several hidden features that make the Pixel 9 Pro experience more enjoyable and efficient. These lesser-known tools can significantly enhance usability and customization options for users who want to make the most of their device.

One of the most useful hidden features is App Cloning, which allows users to run two separate instances of the same app simultaneously. This is especially helpful for individuals who need multiple social media accounts or work and personal messaging apps on the same device.

Another exciting feature is AI-Powered Call Screening, an upgrade to Google's Call Screening function that automatically filters spam calls and provides real-time call transcripts. This means users can see who's calling and why before picking up, reducing interruptions from telemarketers or unknown numbers.

Private Space Mode is another notable addition, allowing users to hide specific apps, files, and notifications behind a secure fingerprint-locked section of the phone. This is ideal for storing confidential data, banking apps, or personal media files that require an extra layer of privacy.

Google has also introduced Live Translate Enhancements, which enable real-time language translation across messaging apps, web pages, and voice calls. Whether you're traveling abroad or communicating with someone in a different language, this feature ensures seamless translation and understanding.

For users who frequently record voice notes or meetings, Android 15 includes AI-Powered Voice Summaries, which automatically transcribe and summarize recorded conversations into key points. This is incredibly useful for students, professionals, or anyone who needs to take notes quickly and efficiently.

Mastering Android 15 on the Pixel 9 Pro unlocks a new level of efficiency, customization, and security. The latest updates bring an improved user interface, powerful multitasking capabilities, intelligent AI-driven features, and enhanced privacy tools, ensuring a premium experience for all users.

By learning how to navigate Android 15 effectively, customizing widgets and quick settings, and utilizing hidden features, users can optimize their Pixel 9 Pro for maximum performance and convenience. The Google Pixel 9 Pro is not just a smartphone—it is a powerful companion designed to streamline everyday tasks, improve productivity, and deliver an unparalleled user experience.

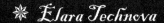

❄ Elara Technova

AI-Powered Camera Features

The Google Pixel 9 Pro boasts one of the most advanced smartphone camera systems to date, combining cutting-edge AI technology with hardware improvements to deliver professional-quality photos and videos. With its triple-lens camera setup, improved computational photography tools, and AI-enhanced stabilization, the Pixel 9 Pro makes photography effortless for both casual users and professional creators. This chapter explores the triple-lens camera system, AI-powered photo editing tools, low-light photography capabilities, and advanced video recording features, ensuring you make the most out of the Pixel 9 Pro's powerful camera system.

Understanding the Triple-Lens Camera System

The Pixel 9 Pro is equipped with a versatile triple-lens rear camera system, each lens designed to handle different photography needs. The primary 50MP wide sensor captures sharp, high-resolution images, ensuring crisp details and true-to-life colors in all lighting conditions. The ultra-wide 48MP lens provides a wider field of view, perfect for landscape shots, group photos, and architectural photography. Lastly, the periscope-style 48MP telephoto lens enables superior optical zoom, allowing you to capture distant objects with remarkable clarity.

One of the key benefits of Google's AI-driven photography approach is the seamless lens-switching technology, which ensures that users can transition between different focal lengths smoothly without losing image quality. The Pixel 9 Pro's AI system automatically selects the best lens for each scenario, optimizing focus, exposure, and white balance in real-time. Additionally, Google's advanced image processing algorithms reduce noise, sharpen details, and balance colors dynamically, creating a professional-quality output straight from the camera.

For portrait lovers, the Pixel 9 Pro's Portrait Mode has been upgraded to deliver better background blur (bokeh effect), natural skin tones, and enhanced edge detection. Thanks to Google's machine learning algorithms, the Pixel 9 Pro can intelligently differentiate subjects from backgrounds, producing a highly realistic depth-of-field effect. Whether you are capturing people, pets, or objects, the AI-powered Portrait Mode ensures studio-quality shots with minimal effort.

Using Magic Editor and Photo Unblur Tools

Google's Magic Editor and Photo Unblur tools have revolutionized smartphone photo editing, making it easier than ever to fix imperfections, enhance details, and reposition subjects within an image. With AI-powered processing, users can edit photos directly on the Pixel 9 Pro without needing third-party editing apps.

The Magic Editor is one of the most powerful AI-driven tools introduced by Google. It allows users to rearrange elements in a photo, remove unwanted objects, adjust lighting, and even alter the background with just a few taps. Whether you want to move a person to the center of the frame, erase distractions, or modify the sky for a more dramatic effect, the Magic Editor uses generative AI to reconstruct missing parts of an image seamlessly. This feature is particularly useful for fixing poorly framed shots, enhancing old photos, or improving the composition of an image without needing professional editing skills.

The Photo Unblur tool is another game-changer, especially for capturing fast-moving subjects or fixing blurry shots. Using Google's AI algorithms, Photo Unblur sharpens out-of-focus images, restores clarity to motion-blurred photos, and enhances fine details automatically. This feature is invaluable for improving nighttime shots, recovering details in shaky photos, and refining images taken in low-light conditions.

Additionally, Google's AI editing suite includes tools like Face Unblur, Real Tone adjustments, and HDR+ optimization, ensuring that every photo taken with the Pixel 9 Pro maintains lifelike colors, sharp details, and balanced contrast. These AI enhancements make the Pixel 9 Pro's camera one of the most powerful smartphone photography tools available today.

Best Settings for Low-Light and Night Sight Photography

Low-light photography has always been a strong suit for Pixel devices, and with the Pixel 9 Pro, Google has further refined Night Sight and AI-powered exposure optimization. Whether you're capturing city lights, nighttime portraits, or starry skies, the Pixel 9 Pro excels in low-light environments.

The Night Sight mode uses advanced computational photography techniques to brighten images, enhance details, and reduce noise in dark environments. Unlike traditional night photography, which often requires long exposure times and a tripod, Night Sight on the Pixel 9

Pro can produce sharp, vibrant, and well-exposed images with minimal effort. By capturing multiple frames at different exposure levels and intelligently combining them, the Pixel 9 Pro can create a final image with rich details, balanced highlights, and deep shadows.

For the best low-light shots, follow these settings and techniques:

- Enable Night Sight Mode Automatically – The Pixel 9 Pro detects low-light conditions and activates Night Sight without needing manual input. However, you can also turn it on manually in the camera settings for better control.
- Use a Steady Hand or Tripod for Long Exposure Shots – While Google's AI stabilization reduces shake, using a tripod ensures even better results, especially for astrophotography and long-exposure night shots.
- Adjust the Exposure Slider Manually – For creative night photography, adjusting the brightness slider can help you control how much light is captured in a shot, allowing for more dramatic effects.
- Utilize Astrophotography Mode for Stunning Night Skies – If you love capturing stars, galaxies, and the Milky Way, the Astrophotography mode on the Pixel 9 Pro can take long-exposure shots with incredible clarity and detail.

Capturing Stunning 4K Videos with AI Stabilization

The Pixel 9 Pro's video recording capabilities have been significantly enhanced, offering 4K video recording at 60fps, cinematic stabilization, and AI-powered video processing. Whether you're shooting travel vlogs, family moments, or professional content, the Pixel 9 Pro delivers ultra-smooth, high-quality videos.

One of the standout features is AI-powered video stabilization, which helps eliminate shaky footage, motion blur, and focus inconsistencies. Using Google's advanced motion-tracking algorithms, the Pixel 9 Pro ensures that video remains steady even when recording while walking or moving. This is particularly beneficial for action shots, handheld recordings, and live events.

For the best 4K video recording experience, consider these settings and techniques:

- Use Cinematic Mode for Professional-Quality Footage – The Cinematic Mode on the Pixel 9 Pro creates a shallow depth-of-field effect, mimicking the look of high-end cameras by blurring the background and focusing on the subject.
- Enable AI-Enhanced HDR for Better Dynamic Range – HDR Video ensures that highlights and shadows remain well-balanced, even in difficult lighting conditions.

- Record in 60fps for Smoother Motion Capture – If you're shooting sports, action scenes, or fast-moving subjects, recording at 60fps delivers smoother, more natural motion clarity.
- Use Audio Zoom for Clearer Sound Focus – The Pixel 9 Pro's AI-enhanced microphones can focus on specific audio sources while reducing background noise, making it ideal for interviews, vlogs, and professional recordings.

With Google's AI-powered video enhancements, the Pixel 9 Pro ensures that every recorded moment is crisp, stable, and visually stunning, making it an ideal device for both casual users and content creators.

The Pixel 9 Pro's AI-powered camera system takes smartphone photography and videography to new heights, combining hardware excellence with software intelligence. Whether you're capturing high-resolution stills, shooting cinematic videos, or enhancing old photos with AI tools, the Pixel 9 Pro makes it effortless. By leveraging features like Magic Editor, Photo Unblur, Night Sight, and AI stabilization, users can produce professional-grade content without the need for expensive camera equipment.

Elara Technova

Google Assistant and AI Features

The Google Pixel 9 Pro is equipped with one of the most advanced AI-driven virtual assistants, designed to enhance productivity, simplify daily tasks, and provide a seamless hands-free experience. With deep integration into the Pixel ecosystem, Google Assistant goes beyond basic voice commands, offering AI-generated responses, contextual smart replies, real-time translations, and enhanced call management features. This chapter will guide you through setting up and customizing Google Assistant, utilizing AI-powered responses, making the most of voice commands, and leveraging hands-free capabilities for a smarter, more efficient user experience.

Setting Up and Customizing Google Assistant

Setting up Google Assistant on the Pixel 9 Pro is straightforward and allows for extensive customization to tailor the experience to your needs. When you first turn on your device, Google Assistant will prompt you to activate voice recognition, link your Google account, and grant necessary permissions. If you skipped the setup process, you can easily enable it through the Google Assistant settings under the Google app or device settings menu.

Once activated, users can personalize their Google Assistant experience by adjusting various settings, such as choosing a preferred voice, enabling proactive suggestions, setting default apps for commands, and configuring Assistant Routines. Customization options include:

- Changing the Assistant's Voice and Speech Speed – Users can select different voices and even adjust how fast or slow responses are spoken.

- Setting Up Personal Results – Enabling personal results allows Assistant to provide customized recommendations, reminders, and search results based on your usage.
- Enabling Continued Conversation Mode – This feature lets you speak multiple commands without needing to say "Hey Google" repeatedly, making interactions smoother and more natural.
- Customizing News, Weather, and Notifications – You can configure Google Assistant to provide daily updates, briefings, and personalized notifications on traffic, weather, and news based on your interests.

The Pixel 9 Pro's AI capabilities make Google Assistant more intuitive and responsive than ever, allowing users to access information, manage their day, and control their device efficiently.

AI-Generated Responses and Smart Reply

One of the most powerful AI-driven enhancements on the Pixel 9 Pro is AI-generated responses and Smart Reply suggestions. These features help speed up communication and provide intelligent, context-aware suggestions for text-based conversations, emails, and messaging apps.

The Smart Reply feature predicts responses based on the context of the conversation, allowing users to respond with a single tap without needing to type a full message. For instance, if someone asks, "Are we still meeting at 3 PM?" your Pixel 9 Pro will generate response options like "Yes, see you then!" or "Let me check and get back to you." This feature is available across Google Messages, Gmail, and third-party messaging apps that support Google's AI-powered reply system.

Beyond text, Google Assistant's AI-generated responses can also help with:

- Summarizing long emails or messages and suggesting key points to reply to.
- Auto-generating text for emails, messages, or notes based on the context of your conversation.
- Providing contextual actions, such as "Add to Calendar," "Set Reminder," or "Call Back" directly from a message notification.

Additionally, the Pixel 9 Pro leverages AI to detect and suggest emojis, GIFs, and stickers based on the tone and content of your message, making conversations more engaging and expressive.

Voice Commands for Productivity and Smart Home Control

Google Assistant is designed to be a powerful voice-activated tool for productivity and home automation. With voice commands, you can schedule meetings, set reminders, send texts, make calls, open apps, and even control smart home devices—all without touching your phone.

Here are some of the most useful voice commands to streamline tasks:

- Productivity Commands:
    - "Hey Google, set a reminder for my meeting at 10 AM."
    - "Hey Google, read my emails from today."
    - "Hey Google, take a note and save it to Google Keep."
    - "Hey Google, create a to-do list and add 'buy groceries' to it."
- Communication Commands:
    - "Hey Google, text Mom 'I'm on my way'."
    - "Hey Google, call Alex on speaker."
    - "Hey Google, send an email to John with the subject 'Project Update'."
- Navigation and Travel Commands:

- "Hey Google, give me directions to the nearest gas station."
- "Hey Google, how's the traffic to work?"
- "Hey Google, book me a ride to the airport using Uber."
- Smart Home Control:
  - "Hey Google, turn off the living room lights."
  - "Hey Google, set the thermostat to 72 degrees."
  - "Hey Google, lock the front door."
  - "Hey Google, play music on my smart speaker."

With the Pixel 9 Pro's enhanced AI and deep integration with Google Home and smart devices, you can seamlessly manage your smart home, schedule your day, and stay organized with simple voice commands.

Hands-Free Features and Call Screening

A standout feature of the Pixel 9 Pro is its advanced hands-free capabilities, designed to reduce distractions and enhance accessibility. With Google Assistant's hands-free controls, users can answer calls, interact with notifications, and even dictate messages without needing to physically touch their phone.

One of the most impressive hands-free features is Google's Call Screening, which uses AI-powered voice recognition to identify spam calls, filter robocalls, and even transcribe unknown caller responses in real time. When an unknown number calls, you can let Google Assistant answer for you, display the transcribed response, and decide whether to take the call or decline it.

For users who frequently use voice controls, Google Assistant's "Read Aloud" feature allows it to read out incoming messages, emails, or web pages, making it convenient for those on the go. Additionally, the voice dictation tool has been improved with faster processing and higher accuracy, allowing you to compose messages, write notes, or dictate documents with ease.

Another hands-free enhancement is Google Assistant's "Voice Access" feature, which enables users to control their phone with voice commands. This is especially useful for accessing apps, adjusting settings, or launching actions when the phone is out of reach. Some practical commands include:

- "Hey Google, turn on Do Not Disturb."

- "Hey Google, take a selfie."
- "Hey Google, start a timer for 10 minutes."
- "Hey Google, turn on dark mode."

The Google Pixel 9 Pro's AI-driven features and Google Assistant capabilities transform the way users interact with their smartphones. From customizable settings and AI-generated smart replies to powerful voice commands and hands-free call screening, the Pixel 9 Pro ensures a seamless, intelligent, and highly efficient user experience. Whether you need to enhance productivity, simplify communication, control smart home devices, or use voice assistance on the go, the Pixel 9 Pro's Google Assistant integration offers unparalleled convenience and functionality.

※ Elara Technova

Battery Optimization and Charging Solutions

The Google Pixel 9 Pro comes equipped with an advanced battery management system, designed to enhance efficiency, maximize battery life, and support high-speed charging. With the Adaptive Battery feature, power-efficient hardware, and intelligent software optimizations, users can experience longer-lasting battery performance while taking advantage of wireless and fast charging technologies. This chapter provides a detailed breakdown of battery optimization techniques, the best charging methods, and how to monitor battery health to ensure long-term performance.

Understanding the Adaptive Battery Feature

The Adaptive Battery feature on the Pixel 9 Pro is powered by Google's AI-driven system, which learns your app usage patterns and prioritizes power allocation accordingly. This means that the apps you use frequently receive more power, while less frequently used apps are restricted from running in the background to conserve battery.

This feature is always active by default, but users can manually adjust settings under Settings > Battery > Adaptive Preferences. Within this menu, there are several options that allow you to fine-tune power consumption based on your needs:

- Adaptive Charging: This feature slowly charges your Pixel overnight and reaches full charge right before you wake up, reducing battery strain and extending its lifespan.
- Adaptive Battery Mode: This setting reduces power consumption for apps that are not regularly used, preventing unnecessary battery drain.
- Optimized App Standby: Apps that you rarely open will be put into a deep sleep state, ensuring they do not consume battery in the background.

Another important aspect of Adaptive Battery is that it adjusts performance dynamically based on your daily routine. If the system detects that your battery is running low before your usual recharge time, it will automatically reduce power usage by dimming the screen, lowering refresh rates, and limiting background activity.

Best Practices for Wireless and Fast Charging

The Pixel 9 Pro supports both wired and wireless fast charging, allowing users to quickly power up their device without long wait times. However, to ensure safe and efficient charging, it is crucial to follow best practices for maintaining battery health while maximizing charging speeds.

Fast Wired Charging

The Pixel 9 Pro supports 30W wired fast charging, which significantly reduces charging time. To take full advantage of this feature:

- Use Google's official 30W charger or a USB Power Delivery (USB-PD) certified charger to ensure maximum compatibility.
- Plug your phone into a power source with a USB-C to USB-C cable that supports high-speed charging.
- Avoid using third-party chargers that do not meet Google's charging standards, as they may

cause slower charging speeds or battery degradation over time.

- Charge your phone in a cool environment since heat can slow down the charging process and impact battery longevity.

Wireless Charging and Battery Share

The Pixel 9 Pro supports 23W wireless fast charging with Google's Pixel Stand (2nd Gen) and lower speeds with standard Qi-compatible wireless chargers. When using wireless charging, follow these steps:

- Align the phone properly on the charging pad to ensure efficient power transfer.
- Use a certified high-wattage wireless charger for optimal charging speeds.
- Remove thick cases or metal attachments, as they can block wireless charging signals.

Additionally, Battery Share allows the Pixel 9 Pro to wirelessly charge other devices, such as earbuds or smartwatches. To use this feature, go to Settings > Battery > Battery Share, enable the function, and place the other device on the back of the phone.

How to Extend Battery Life Throughout the Day

Even with a powerful battery, it is essential to adopt best practices for daily power management to get the most out of a single charge. Here are effective ways to extend battery life throughout the day:

Optimize Display Settings

- Lower the screen brightness manually or enable Adaptive Brightness under Settings > Display > Adaptive Brightness.
- Reduce the screen timeout duration to prevent unnecessary power consumption.
- Turn off the Always-On Display if you don't need it, as this feature continuously uses battery power.

Manage Connectivity Features

- Turn off Bluetooth, Wi-Fi, and NFC when not in use.
- Use Airplane Mode in low-signal areas, as searching for a network drains the battery.
- Disable 5G when you do not need ultra-fast data speeds, as it consumes more power than LTE.

Limit Background App Activity

- Use Battery Saver Mode under Settings > Battery > Battery Saver to restrict background processes.
- Close unused apps and disable auto-sync for unnecessary services.
- Uninstall apps that run in the background and consume excessive power.

Smart Charging Habits

- Avoid letting the battery drain below 10% too often, as deep discharges can shorten its lifespan.
- Keep your battery level between 20% and 80% for optimal health.
- Do not leave your phone plugged in overnight, as this may cause long-term battery wear.

By following these steps, you can ensure that your Pixel 9 Pro remains powered throughout the day while maintaining battery health over time.

Monitoring Battery Usage and Power-Saving Modes

Google provides several tools within Android 15 to help monitor battery performance and track power consumption. Users can access detailed insights under Settings > Battery > Battery Usage, where they will find a breakdown of which apps and features are using the most battery.

Battery Usage Breakdown

The Battery Usage section provides:

- A graph showing battery consumption over time.
- A list of apps ranked by battery usage, allowing users to identify power-hungry applications.
- Real-time tracking of screen-on time, background processes, and system usage.

If an app is consuming an abnormal amount of battery, you can:

- Force stop the app under Settings > Apps > Select the app > Force Stop.
- Restrict background activity by selecting App Battery Usage > Restricted.
- Uninstall the app if it is not essential.

Using Battery Saver and Extreme Battery Saver

The Battery Saver Mode helps extend battery life by limiting performance, reducing background activity, and turning off non-essential services. To enable it:

- Go to Settings > Battery > Battery Saver and toggle it on.
- Schedule Battery Saver to activate automatically when the battery drops below a certain percentage.

For extreme situations, Extreme Battery Saver Mode turns off almost all background activities, allowing only essential apps to run. This mode is useful when traveling, during emergencies, or when you need your phone to last as long as possible.

The Google Pixel 9 Pro's battery optimization features, combined with fast and wireless charging capabilities, provide users with long-lasting battery performance and flexibility. By leveraging Adaptive Battery, implementing smart charging habits, and utilizing power-saving tools, users can ensure their device stays powered efficiently throughout the day. Whether you are a heavy gamer, a business professional, or an everyday user, these battery optimization techniques will help maximize performance, reduce charging time, and prolong battery lifespan.

Connectivity and Networking

The Google Pixel 9 Pro is designed with cutting-edge connectivity features, allowing users to experience ultra-fast internet speeds, seamless wireless connections, and advanced data-sharing capabilities. With 5G compatibility, Wi-Fi 7 support, Bluetooth enhancements, and NFC functionality, the Pixel 9 Pro is built for modern connectivity needs. This chapter provides a detailed guide on how to maximize network performance, connect to various devices, and utilize advanced wireless features.

Setting Up 5G for Maximum Speed

The Google Pixel 9 Pro supports 5G connectivity, delivering blazing-fast internet speeds, lower latency, and improved network stability. To fully utilize 5G, users must ensure that their carrier supports 5G and that their mobile plan includes 5G access.

Enabling 5G on the Pixel 9 Pro

To activate 5G connectivity, follow these steps:

- Open the Settings app and go to Network & Internet.
- Tap Mobile Network, then select Preferred Network Type.
- Choose 5G/LTE/3G/2G (Auto) to allow the device to connect to the best available network.

If 5G is not working or not appearing as an option, consider these troubleshooting tips:

- Check carrier compatibility: Not all carriers support 5G in every region. Visit your carrier's website to confirm 5G coverage.

- Ensure your SIM card is 5G-enabled: If you're using an old SIM card, you may need to upgrade to a new one.
- Restart your phone: Sometimes, simply rebooting the device helps the network recognize the 5G signal.
- Check for software updates: Google frequently rolls out network optimizations, so always update to the latest firmware.

Maximizing 5G Performance

For the best 5G experience:

- Use 5G in areas with strong signal coverage, as weak 5G signals may drain the battery faster.
- Disable 5G in low-signal areas to conserve battery life. You can manually switch to LTE mode when 5G isn't necessary.
- Monitor data usage, as 5G speeds can consume large amounts of data quickly. If on a limited plan, set data limits under Settings > Network & Internet > Data Usage.

Wi-Fi 7: What You Need to Know

The Google Pixel 9 Pro is Wi-Fi 7 compatible, offering faster speeds, lower latency, and better network efficiency. Wi-Fi 7 provides a significant upgrade over previous Wi-Fi generations, making streaming, gaming, and video conferencing smoother and more reliable.

Setting Up Wi-Fi 7 on the Pixel 9 Pro

- Open Settings and go to Network & Internet.
- Select Wi-Fi, then choose the fastest available network.
- If your router supports Wi-Fi 7, your device will automatically connect to the highest speed available.

Benefits of Wi-Fi 7

- Ultra-fast speeds for streaming in 4K and 8K, gaming, and large file downloads.
- Lower latency, reducing lag when making video calls or playing online games.
- Increased efficiency, allowing multiple devices to connect without slowing down performance.

Optimizing Wi-Fi Performance

- Place your router in an open space for better signal strength.
- Use a dual-band router that supports 2.4GHz and 6GHz for a stable connection.
- Keep your Wi-Fi software updated for improved security and speed.

If Wi-Fi 7 isn't available in your home, you can still benefit from Wi-Fi 6 or 6E, which also delivers great speeds.

Bluetooth and Pairing with Wireless Accessories

The Google Pixel 9 Pro features the latest Bluetooth technology, allowing for seamless pairing with headphones, speakers, smartwatches, and other wireless accessories.

Pairing a Bluetooth Device

- Open Settings and go to Connected Devices.
- Tap Pair New Device and select the accessory from the list.
- Confirm the pairing request on both devices and complete the connection.

Once paired, the device will automatically reconnect when in range, unless manually disconnected.

Optimizing Bluetooth Connectivity

- Ensure your accessories are in pairing mode before connecting.
- Avoid interference by keeping Bluetooth devices away from crowded Wi-Fi signals.
- Use Bluetooth LE (Low Energy) to reduce battery drain when connected to smart devices.

Common Bluetooth troubleshooting tips include restarting Bluetooth, resetting paired devices, and updating firmware on both the Pixel 9 Pro and connected accessories.

Using NFC for Contactless Payments and File Transfers

Near Field Communication (NFC) is an essential feature of the Pixel 9 Pro, enabling fast and secure contactless payments, file transfers, and smart device pairing.

Setting Up Google Pay for Contactless Payments

- Open Google Wallet and sign in with your Google account.
- Add a payment card by selecting Payment Methods > Add Card.
- Follow on-screen instructions to verify the card with your bank.
- Enable Tap to Pay in Settings > Connected Devices > NFC.

To make a contactless payment, simply hold your phone near a payment terminal with the screen unlocked. You'll receive a confirmation once the payment is processed.

Transferring Files with Android Beam and Nearby Share

- Enable Nearby Share under Settings > Connected Devices.
- Select the file you want to share, tap the Share button, and choose Nearby Share.
- Hold the receiving device close to your phone to complete the transfer.

This method is useful for quickly sharing photos, contacts, and documents without using an internet connection.

The Google Pixel 9 Pro offers an advanced suite of connectivity features, ensuring fast, seamless, and secure network performance. With 5G speeds, Wi-Fi 7 support, Bluetooth enhancements, and NFC-powered contactless interactions, the device is designed to keep users connected anywhere, anytime. By properly setting up and optimizing these features, users can enjoy faster internet, better Bluetooth experiences, and quick contactless transactions.

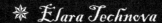
❋ Elara Technova

Personalizing Your Pixel Experience

The Google Pixel 9 Pro is designed for maximum customization, allowing users to tailor the interface, sounds, accessibility options, and user profiles to suit their needs. With a variety of themes, icon packs, wallpapers, and sound settings, users can create a personalized experience that makes their device truly unique. This chapter provides a detailed step-by-step guide on how to modify the Pixel 9 Pro's appearance, customize notification and ringtone sounds, optimize accessibility features, and set up multiple user profiles for shared use.

Changing Themes, Icons, and Wallpapers

Customizing the visual appearance of the Pixel 9 Pro helps users create a unique and visually appealing interface that matches their personality or mood. Google's Material You design allows for deep customization, ensuring that colors and themes adapt dynamically to your wallpaper selection.

Changing Themes and Colors

Google's Android 15 enables dynamic theming, which automatically adjusts the system colors based on the chosen wallpaper. To customize:

- Open Settings and navigate to Wallpaper & Style.
- Select Color Palette to adjust system colors, including the notification shade and app icons.
- Choose Wallpaper Colors to match the system's color scheme to your wallpaper or select Basic Colors for a uniform look.

Customizing App Icons and Fonts

- **Icon Shapes & Sizes**: Google allows users to modify icon shapes and sizes. Navigate to Settings > Wallpaper & Style > Themed Icons to apply a uniform style to app icons.
- **Changing Fonts & Text Size**: Adjusting font style and text size can improve readability. Go to Settings > Display > Font Size & Style to select from available options.
- **Icon Packs from Google Play Store**: Users who prefer a completely different look can download third-party icon packs for a fresh and unique home screen layout.

Selecting a New Wallpaper

Changing the wallpaper enhances the phone's aesthetics. To update the background:

- Long-press on the home screen and tap Wallpaper & Style.
- Browse through Live Wallpapers, Photos, and Default Images.
- Choose an image and tap Set Wallpaper to apply it to the home or lock screen.

Live wallpapers add motion and interactivity, while static wallpapers provide a cleaner and battery-efficient look.

The Google Pixel 9 Pro offers various built-in sound options, and users can also upload custom ringtones and notification sounds to make alerts more personal.

Changing Ringtones

- Open Settings and go to Sound & Vibration.
- Tap Phone Ringtone and choose from the list of available sounds.
- To set a custom ringtone, tap Add Ringtone, select a downloaded audio file, and confirm.

For those who want unique caller tones, apps like Zedge allow users to download personalized ringtones.

Customizing Notification and Alarm Sounds

- Go to Settings > Sound & Vibration > Default Notification Sound.
- Choose from the built-in tones or select a custom sound file.
- For alarms, navigate to Clock App > Alarm Sound and pick a preferred tune.

Tip: Avoid using long or loud notification sounds to prevent distractions. Opt for softer tones for a more pleasant user experience.

The Pixel 9 Pro includes a variety of accessibility features to assist users with vision, hearing, and mobility impairments. These options enhance usability and ensure the phone is comfortable for all users.

Vision Accessibility Options

- Magnification Gestures: Users can zoom into any part of the screen by enabling Magnification in Settings > Accessibility > Magnification.
- High-Contrast Mode: Improves text visibility by increasing the contrast between text and background. Activate it under Settings > Accessibility > Text & Display.
- TalkBack: This feature reads aloud on-screen text for users with visual impairments. Activate it via Settings > Accessibility > TalkBack.

Hearing Accessibility Features

- Live Caption: Automatically generates real-time subtitles for videos and voice recordings. Turn it on in Settings > Accessibility > Live Caption.
- Hearing Aid Support: Connect Bluetooth-enabled hearing aids for direct audio transmission from the device. Go to Settings > Connected Devices > Hearing Devices.

One-Handed Mode for Easier Navigation

The Pixel 9 Pro is a large device, but One-Handed Mode makes it easier to operate using just one hand. To enable:

- Go to Settings > System > Gestures > One-Handed Mode.
- Enable Use One-Handed Mode.
- Swipe down on the gesture navigation bar to bring the screen lower for easier reach.

Creating Multiple User Profiles

If the Pixel 9 Pro is shared among multiple users, setting up user profiles allows each person to have a separate experience with personalized apps, settings, and storage space.

Adding a New User Profile

- Open Settings > System > Multiple Users.
- Toggle Allow Multiple Users to enable the feature.
- Tap Add User and follow the setup instructions to create a new profile.

Each user profile operates independently, meaning apps, home screen layouts, and preferences remain unique to each user.

Setting Up a Guest Profile

A Guest Mode is useful when temporarily sharing the phone with someone else. It provides limited access to apps and personal data.

- Go to Settings > System > Multiple Users > Guest.
- Activate Guest Mode whenever needed, and reset it after use to clear session data.

This feature ensures privacy and security while allowing shared use of the device.

The Google Pixel 9 Pro is built for maximum customization, allowing users to fine-tune every aspect of the device to match their preferences. Whether it's changing wallpapers, adjusting notification sounds, enabling accessibility features, or setting up multiple user profiles, the Pixel 9 Pro offers a fully personalized experience. Customization not only enhances aesthetics and usability but also improves efficiency and comfort, making the device an extension of the user's style.

Maximizing Google Pixel's Security

S ecurity is one of the most important aspects of owning a smartphone, and Google has built the Pixel 9 Pro with robust security features to protect user data, accounts, and privacy. Whether it's biometric authentication, two-factor security, private browsing settings, or theft protection, the Pixel 9 Pro offers comprehensive security tools that ensure peace of mind for every user. This chapter explores various ways to enhance security, prevent unauthorized access, and safeguard sensitive information.

Setting Up Face Unlock and Fingerprint Scanner

The Google Pixel 9 Pro offers two highly secure biometric authentication options: Face Unlock and Fingerprint Scanner. These features make unlocking the device faster and more convenient while ensuring only the rightful owner can access it.

Enabling Face Unlock

- Open Settings and navigate to Security & Privacy.
- Tap Face Unlock and follow the on-screen instructions.
- Position your face inside the frame and let the device scan from different angles.
- Once complete, enable Unlock Phone to allow Face Unlock to work on the lock screen.

Face Unlock provides fast authentication, but for increased security, it works only in well-lit environments and cannot be used for authorizing banking apps or purchases.

Setting Up the Fingerprint Scanner

The Pixel 9 Pro features an under-display fingerprint scanner, which provides an additional layer of security and can be used for unlocking the phone, apps, and sensitive transactions.

- Go to Settings > Security & Privacy > Fingerprint Unlock.
- Follow the steps to scan your fingerprint multiple times for better accuracy.
- Ensure fingers are dry and clean for best results.

Once set up, the fingerprint sensor can be used to unlock the device instantly, approve Google Play purchases, and authorize banking transactions for an extra layer of protection.

Two-Factor Authentication and Secure Folders

Beyond biometric authentication, Google's Two-Factor Authentication (2FA) and Secure Folders add another level of safety to protect personal data, login credentials, and confidential files.

Setting Up Two-Factor Authentication (2FA) for Google Accounts

- Open the Google Account settings from Settings > Security.
- Navigate to 2-Step Verification and follow the prompts.

- Select a preferred verification method, such as SMS codes, Google Prompts, or Authenticator apps.
- Enable Backup Codes in case the primary authentication method is unavailable.

2FA prevents hackers from accessing a user's Google account, even if they have the password, by requiring a secondary verification method before logging in.

Using Secure Folder to Protect Sensitive Files

The Secure Folder feature helps store confidential photos, documents, and apps in a locked folder that cannot be accessed without authentication. To enable Secure Folder:

- Go to Settings > Security & Privacy > Secure Folder.
- Set up a PIN, pattern, or biometric lock.
- Move sensitive files or apps into the Secure Folder for added protection.

This ensures that personal and work-related files remain private, even if the phone is shared with others.

For enhanced online privacy, Google Pixel 9 Pro provides private browsing options, incognito mode, and detailed app permissions management to protect against unauthorized tracking and data leaks.

Enabling Private Browsing in Chrome

- Open Google Chrome and tap on the three-dot menu.
- Select New Incognito Tab to browse the web without leaving a history.
- Websites and apps won't track activity, ensuring private browsing.

Incognito mode is useful when signing into temporary accounts or accessing sensitive content, as it prevents passwords, cookies, and browsing history from being stored.

Managing App Permissions for Enhanced Privacy

Apps request access to contacts, location, camera, microphone, and storage, but not all of them need full access. To review and restrict app permissions:

- Navigate to Settings > Apps > Permissions Manager.

- Review each app's access to camera, location, storage, and microphone.
- Change permissions to Allow Only While Using the App or Deny for added control.

Limiting app permissions prevents unnecessary tracking and ensures that only trusted applications access sensitive data.

Anti-Theft Features and Find My Device

Losing a smartphone is a stressful experience, but Google's anti-theft tools make it easier to track, lock, and erase data remotely if the device is stolen or misplaced.

Enabling Find My Device

Find My Device is a built-in feature that allows users to locate, lock, or erase their Pixel 9 Pro remotely. To activate:

- Go to Settings > Security & Privacy > Find My Device.
- Enable Use Find My Device to allow remote tracking.
- Visit android.com/find on any browser to locate the phone.

Using Smart Lock for Added Security

Smart Lock keeps the phone unlocked when it's in trusted locations or connected to trusted devices, reducing frequent unlocking while ensuring security. To set up:

- Navigate to Settings > Security & Privacy > Smart Lock.
- Choose from On-Body Detection, Trusted Places, or Trusted Devices.

Locking and Erasing Data Remotely

If the phone is stolen or lost:

- Log into Find My Device from another phone or PC.
- Choose Secure Device to lock the phone remotely.
- If the phone cannot be retrieved, select Erase Device to remove all personal data.

With powerful biometric authentication, two-factor security, private browsing tools, app permission controls, and anti-theft features, the Google Pixel 9 Pro ensures top-level security and privacy protection. Users can enjoy peace of mind knowing that their personal and financial information is well-guarded against unauthorized access, online threats, and theft.

Google Photos and Cloud Storage

The Google Pixel 9 Pro comes with seamless integration with Google Photos and cloud storage services, making it easier to store, organize, and manage digital content without worrying about running out of space. Google Photos offers AI-powered features, such as automatic backup, smart album organization, AI-generated memories, and advanced editing tools that enhance the overall photo and video experience. Additionally, Google's cloud storage solutions ensure that users can free up space on their devices while keeping their files accessible from any device. This chapter explores the best ways to use Google Photos efficiently, manage storage, and keep data safe without losing precious memories.

Using Google Photos for Seamless Backup

Google Photos is the default photo management app on the Pixel 9 Pro, providing a secure and automatic backup for all photos and videos. It ensures that no media files are lost, even if the device is damaged or lost.

Enabling Automatic Backup in Google Photos

- Open the Google Photos app and tap the profile icon in the top-right corner.
- Go to Photos Settings > Backup & Sync.
- Turn on Backup & Sync to upload photos and videos to Google Drive.
- Choose the backup quality:
  - o Original Quality (full resolution, counts toward Google Drive storage).
  - o Storage Saver (slightly compressed, saves space).

With automatic backup enabled, all new photos and videos taken on the Pixel 9 Pro are instantly uploaded to the cloud, making them accessible on any device linked to the user's Google account.

Restoring Photos from Google Photos

If photos are accidentally deleted, they can be recovered from the Trash within 60 days:

- Open Google Photos > Library > Trash.
- Select the deleted photos and tap Restore.

This feature ensures that important memories are never permanently lost unless manually erased.

Organizing Albums and AI-Generated Memories

Google Photos goes beyond simple storage by offering AI-powered organization tools that help users categorize, search, and relive their moments effortlessly.

Creating and Managing Albums

- Open Google Photos and select multiple photos.
- Tap Add to Album and choose to create a new album or add to an existing one.
- Name the album and arrange photos chronologically or by category.

Users can also collaborate on albums, allowing family and friends to add their own photos to shared memories.

Using AI-Generated Memories

Google Photos automatically creates "Memories", grouping photos based on people, places, and events.

- To view AI-generated memories, open Google Photos and check the top section for suggested moments.
- These include "This Day in History", highlighted trips, and special occasions.
- Users can save, share, or remove specific memories from appearing in suggestions.

This feature enhances the photo-viewing experience, making it easier to relive important moments without scrolling through thousands of images manually.

Freeing Up Storage Without Losing Data

One of the biggest challenges for smartphone users is managing storage space efficiently. Google Photos provides tools that allow users to free up local device storage while keeping files accessible online.

Using the "Free Up Space" Feature

- Open Google Photos > Profile Icon > Free Up Space.
- The app will detect and list photos and videos that have already been backed up.
- Tap Delete to remove them from the device but keep them available in the cloud.

This helps clear internal storage without permanently deleting important files.

Compressing Photos to Save Space

If Google Drive is running out of storage, users can convert existing photos to "Storage Saver" quality to reduce file size while keeping them backed up.

- Go to Google Photos > Settings > Backup & Sync > Manage Storage.
- Select Recover Storage to compress all previous uploads to high-quality format.

This feature is useful for users with limited Google Drive storage space but who still want to keep all their images backed up online.

Google Photos integrates with Google Drive and other cloud storage solutions, allowing users to store, sync, and access files across multiple devices.

Linking Google Drive with Google Photos

- Open Google Drive and navigate to Settings > Google Photos Integration.
- Enable "Show Google Photos in Drive" to access photos directly from Drive.

This feature makes it easy to view, organize, and share photos and videos within the Google Drive environment, useful for users who prefer file-based organization.

Syncing Photos Across Devices

Google Photos automatically syncs across phones, tablets, and computers:

- Log in to photos.google.com to access the full library from any device.
- The app ensures that all edits made on one device are reflected across all synced devices.

Users can also download Google Photos for Windows or macOS to manage cloud storage from a desktop or laptop.

The Google Pixel 9 Pro offers one of the best photo and video storage solutions through Google Photos and cloud integration. With automatic backup, AI-powered organization, free storage management tools, and multi-device syncing, users can store their memories safely, optimize device space, and easily retrieve files whenever needed. Whether it's creating albums, recovering lost photos, or managing cloud backups, Google Photos simplifies the experience, making storage effortless and hassle-free.

Best Apps and Tools for Productivity

The Google Pixel 9 Pro is not just a powerful smartphone; it is also a highly efficient productivity tool that can help users manage their work, schedule, and daily tasks with ease. Whether you are a student, a professional, or someone who needs better time management and task organization, the Pixel 9 Pro provides an array of built-in and third-party productivity apps designed to enhance efficiency. From note-taking and scheduling to multitasking and collaboration, this chapter will explore the best apps and tools that can help boost productivity and streamline daily activities.

Must-Have Productivity Apps for Google Pixel

To maximize efficiency, users need the right productivity apps that can help with task management, organization, communication, and collaboration. The Google Pixel 9 Pro comes with pre-installed Google apps that are highly effective, but there are also several third-party apps that can further improve the user experience.

Google Workspace (Docs, Sheets, and Slides)

Google's Workspace suite is an essential set of apps for creating, editing, and collaborating on documents, spreadsheets, and presentations. These cloud-based tools allow users to work on projects from any device, making them ideal for both personal and professional use.

- Google Docs is perfect for writing, editing, and sharing documents in real-time.

- Google Sheets helps users manage data, create reports, and analyze information effectively.
- Google Slides enables the creation of professional presentations that can be shared or presented remotely.

Evernote and Microsoft OneNote

For users who prefer advanced note-taking features, Evernote and OneNote provide organized note storage, audio recording, and document scanning. These apps allow users to save ideas, to-do lists, and meeting notes in a searchable and easily accessible format.

Trello and Asana for Task Management

For professionals managing multiple projects, Trello and Asana are top-rated project management apps that help users organize tasks, set deadlines, and collaborate with teams efficiently.

- Trello uses a drag-and-drop card system to track tasks.
- Asana allows teams to assign responsibilities, set due dates, and monitor progress.

Using these tools ensures that work stays organized, structured, and on schedule.

Google Keep is one of the most underrated but powerful productivity apps for the Pixel 9 Pro. It offers a simple yet highly effective way to take quick notes, set reminders, and create checklists.

Creating and Managing Notes in Google Keep

- Open Google Keep and tap the plus icon to create a new note.
- Type in important thoughts, meeting points, or quick memos.
- Color-code and label notes for better organization.

Users can attach images, voice recordings, and handwritten notes, making Google Keep an excellent tool for capturing ideas instantly.

Setting Reminders with Google Keep

Google Keep allows users to set time-based or location-based reminders:

- Time-based reminders notify users at a specific time, helping them stay on schedule.
- Location-based reminders trigger notifications when arriving at a certain place, such as reminding you to buy groceries when near a store.

These reminders ensure that important tasks and deadlines are never forgotten.

Managing Tasks with Google Calendar and Tasks

A well-organized calendar system is crucial for productivity, efficiency, and time management. The Google Pixel 9 Pro integrates Google Calendar and Google Tasks, allowing users to schedule events, track deadlines, and manage daily responsibilities seamlessly.

Using Google Calendar for Scheduling

- Open Google Calendar and tap the plus icon to add an event.
- Set a title, date, time, and location.
- Add reminders and notifications to ensure the event is not missed.
- Invite others via email for team meetings, work appointments, or social gatherings.

Syncing Google Tasks with Google Calendar

Google Tasks integrates with Google Calendar, allowing users to track daily responsibilities alongside scheduled events.

- Open Google Calendar and tap Tasks.
- Add to-do lists and assign due dates.

97

- Drag and drop tasks to different dates for better scheduling.

By using Google Calendar and Tasks together, users can prioritize workload efficiently and manage their time more effectively.

Multitasking with Split-Screen Mode

The Pixel 9 Pro's large OLED display and powerful processing capabilities make multitasking effortless. The split-screen feature allows users to use two apps at the same time, enhancing productivity.

How to Enable Split-Screen Mode

- Open an app that supports split-screen functionality.
- Swipe up from the bottom and tap the app switcher button.
- Tap the three-dot menu on the app's window and select Split screen.
- Choose the second app to open in the lower half of the screen.

Best Use Cases for Split-Screen Mode

- Taking notes while watching a lecture or webinar.
- Comparing two documents side by side.

- Browsing emails while chatting on a messaging app.

This feature enhances multitasking capabilities, allowing users to stay productive without constantly switching between apps.

The Google Pixel 9 Pro is designed to be a powerful productivity tool, providing users with advanced task management apps, seamless note-taking tools, calendar integration, and multitasking features. By leveraging the best Google productivity apps and third-party tools, users can streamline their workflow, increase efficiency, and stay organized. Whether it's scheduling meetings, setting reminders, or working on multiple tasks simultaneously, the Pixel 9 Pro makes productivity effortless.

Elara Technova

Troubleshooting and Common Issues

The Google Pixel 9 Pro is designed to provide a smooth, efficient, and seamless user experience, but like any electronic device, it may occasionally encounter technical issues that can disrupt performance. Whether it's Wi-Fi connectivity problems, overheating concerns, app crashes, or performance slowdowns, understanding how to troubleshoot and resolve these problems is essential for maintaining a fully functional device. This chapter covers common issues that users may face with the Pixel 9 Pro and provides detailed, step-by-step solutions to address these concerns effectively.

Fixing Wi-Fi and Connectivity Problems

One of the most frustrating issues for any smartphone user is Wi-Fi or cellular network problems. If your Google Pixel 9 Pro is experiencing slow internet speeds, frequent disconnections, or difficulty connecting to networks, there are several troubleshooting steps that can help resolve these issues.

Checking Basic Network Settings

Before diving into advanced troubleshooting, ensure that the issue isn't due to a simple misconfiguration.

- Go to Settings > Network & Internet > Wi-Fi and verify that Wi-Fi is turned on and connected to the correct network.
- If using mobile data, ensure that Airplane Mode is off and that Mobile Data is enabled under Settings > Network & Internet > Mobile Network.
- Restart your router and modem if the problem persists, as network congestion or temporary malfunctions may be affecting connectivity.

Resetting Network Settings

If connectivity issues continue, resetting the network settings can resolve hidden issues related to Wi-Fi, Bluetooth, or cellular connections.

- Navigate to Settings > System > Reset options > Reset Wi-Fi, mobile & Bluetooth.
- Confirm and allow the device to reset network settings before reconnecting to Wi-Fi.

If problems persist, check with your internet service provider (ISP) or mobile carrier to ensure there are no service outages in your area.

Resolving Overheating Issues

Overheating is a common issue for smartphones, especially those with high-performance processors like the Tensor G4 chip. The Google Pixel 9 Pro is built with advanced thermal management, but prolonged gaming, camera use, or high-resolution video streaming may cause excessive heat.

Common Causes of Overheating

- Running multiple high-performance apps at the same time.
- Playing graphically intensive games for extended periods.
- Using the phone while charging, especially with fast charging enabled.
- Keeping the phone in direct sunlight or in a hot environment.

Steps to Prevent Overheating

- Close background apps that are consuming processing power. Go to Settings > Apps > Running Apps and manually close unnecessary apps.
- Reduce the screen brightness and turn on adaptive brightness to prevent excessive heat buildup.
- Enable Battery Saver Mode under Settings > Battery to limit background activity and reduce power consumption.
- If overheating occurs while charging, switch to a standard charger instead of a fast charger and ensure that the phone is placed in a cool, ventilated area.

If the device becomes extremely hot, power it off immediately and allow it to cool down before resuming use.

Fixing App Crashes and Performance Glitches

Occasionally, apps may freeze, crash, or fail to open, causing frustration for users. Performance glitches can also slow down navigation, making the device less responsive. Here are a few effective ways to troubleshoot and fix these issues.

Clearing Cache and Data for Problematic Apps

- Go to Settings > Apps > See all apps and select the app that is frequently crashing.
- Tap Storage & cache, then Clear cache.
- If the issue persists, tap Clear data to reset the app completely (note that this will erase saved settings in the app).

Updating Apps and the Operating System

- Open the Google Play Store, tap your profile icon, and go to Manage apps & device to check for pending updates.
- Ensure your Google Pixel 9 Pro is running the latest version of Android by navigating to Settings > System > Software Update.

Restarting or Booting into Safe Mode

If an app continues to misbehave, try restarting your device or booting into Safe Mode, which temporarily disables all third-party apps.

- Press and hold the Power button, then tap and hold the Restart option until you see Reboot to Safe Mode.
- In Safe Mode, check if the app functions properly. If it does, the issue might be due to a conflicting third-party app.

When to Perform a Factory Reset

If persistent issues such as frequent crashes, severe lag, or unresponsive system behavior remain unresolved after all troubleshooting steps, performing a factory reset may be necessary. A factory reset erases all data and restores the device to its original state, eliminating deep-rooted software bugs.

Steps to Perform a Factory Reset

- Navigate to Settings > System > Reset options.
- Select Erase all data (factory reset).
- Confirm the reset and allow the Pixel 9 Pro to restart with factory settings.

Important Considerations Before Resetting

- Back up important data using Google One, Google Drive, or an external storage option.
- Ensure your device is fully charged or connected to power before initiating the reset.
- After resetting, you will need to reconfigure your Google account and reinstall apps.

A factory reset should be considered as a last resort, only when all other troubleshooting methods fail to resolve the problem.

The Google Pixel 9 Pro is a highly optimized smartphone, but like all tech devices, it may experience occasional issues related to connectivity, overheating, performance, and software bugs. By following these detailed troubleshooting steps, users can resolve most problems without seeking professional assistance. Understanding how to fix network problems, prevent overheating, restore app functionality, and reset the device when needed ensures a smooth and frustration-free user experience.

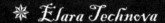
✳ Elara Technova

Google Pixel and Smart Home Integration

The Google Pixel 9 Pro is more than just a smartphone; it is a powerful hub for controlling smart home devices. With the seamless integration of Google Home, Nest devices, and Google Assistant, users can manage everything from lighting, security systems, thermostats, and entertainment centers with simple voice commands or taps on the screen. This chapter explores how to connect, configure, and automate your smart home ecosystem using the Pixel 9 Pro, ensuring a more convenient, efficient, and connected lifestyle.

Using Pixel 9 Pro to Control Smart Home Devices

The Google Pixel 9 Pro acts as a central control system for all Google-compatible smart home devices, allowing users to adjust lighting, change thermostat settings, monitor security cameras, and control appliances remotely. The Google Home app is the key to managing connected devices, providing an intuitive interface for device control and automation.

To start, users should download and install the Google Home app from the Google Play Store. Once installed, open the app and link compatible smart devices by following the on-screen prompts. Supported devices include smart bulbs, door locks, speakers, TVs, thermostats, security cameras, and more. The Pixel 9 Pro ensures real-time communication with these devices via Wi-Fi, Bluetooth, and NFC, enabling smooth and instant control.

Voice commands using Google Assistant provide hands-free convenience. For instance, saying "Hey Google, turn off the living room lights" or "Set the thermostat to 72 degrees" will execute the commands without the need to open an app. The Pixel 9 Pro's AI-driven speech recognition ensures quick and accurate responses, making smart home control effortless and efficient.

Setting Up Google Home and Nest Integration

Google's Nest ecosystem provides an advanced smart home experience, allowing users to integrate their Pixel 9 Pro with Nest Hub, Nest Audio, Nest Thermostat, and Nest Security Cameras. This setup enhances home automation, voice control, and security monitoring.

To set up Google Home and Nest devices with the Pixel 9 Pro, follow these steps:

1. Open the Google Home app on the Pixel 9 Pro.
2. Tap the "+" icon and select Set up device.
3. Choose Works with Google for third-party smart home products or Set up new device for Nest-branded devices.
4. Follow the on-screen prompts to connect devices to the same Wi-Fi network.
5. Assign devices to specific rooms for easy voice control (e.g., "Living Room Lights" or "Bedroom Speaker").

Once integrated, users can check live security feeds from Nest Cameras, control room temperatures with

Nest Thermostats, and automate routines like turning off lights when leaving home. The Pixel 9 Pro's advanced AI algorithms make these interactions smoother by learning user habits and preferences over time.

Automating Smart Routines with Google Assistant

Automation is a key feature of smart home integration, allowing users to schedule or trigger actions based on specific conditions. With Google Assistant on the Pixel 9 Pro, users can set up routines that activate multiple smart devices simultaneously, enhancing convenience and efficiency.

For example, users can create a "Good Morning" routine that:

- Turns on the bedroom lights.
- Adjusts the thermostat to a comfortable temperature.
- Reads out the daily weather and calendar schedule.
- Starts playing a morning news briefing or favorite music playlist.

Similarly, a "Bedtime" routine **can:**

- Dim or turn off the lights.
- Lock the doors and activate security cameras.
- Turn off the TV and entertainment systems.
- Enable "Do Not Disturb" mode on the Pixel 9 Pro to prevent notifications from interrupting sleep.

To create these routines:

1. Open the Google Home app.
2. Tap Routines and select New Routine.
3. Set a trigger phrase (e.g., "Hey Google, I'm home" or "Hey Google, good night").
4. Choose actions for multiple smart devices.
5. Save and activate the routine for automated control.

These smart routines not only save time but also optimize home energy consumption by ensuring that unused devices are turned off automatically.

Troubleshooting Smart Home Connectivity Issues

While Google Pixel 9 Pro's smart home integration is designed for a seamless experience, occasional connectivity issues may arise. If a smart device fails to respond, there are several troubleshooting steps users can take.

Check Internet and Wi-Fi Connection

- Ensure that all smart devices and the Pixel 9 Pro are connected to the same Wi-Fi network.
- Restart the router and modem to refresh network settings.
- Move smart home devices closer to the Wi-Fi router to improve signal strength.

Reconnect the Device to Google Home

- Open the Google Home app, find the problematic device, and tap "Remove Device".
- Restart the Pixel 9 Pro and smart device, then re-add the device to Google Home.

Update Firmware and Google Home App

- Ensure that the Google Home app and all smart devices are running the latest firmware updates.
- Go to Settings > System > Software Update on the Pixel 9 Pro to check for available updates.

Reset the Smart Device

- If issues persist, reset the smart device to factory settings and set it up from scratch using the Google Home app.
- Refer to the manufacturer's instructions for resetting individual devices like smart bulbs, locks, and cameras.

The Google Pixel 9 Pro is an indispensable tool for smart home automation, offering seamless control over connected devices. With the Google Home app, Nest integration, and Google Assistant-powered routines, users can create a fully automated, voice-controlled home experience. By following the setup guides, automation tips, and troubleshooting solutions in this chapter, users can enhance home security, convenience, and energy efficiency, making the Pixel 9 Pro a true smart home companion.

Using the Pixel 9 Pro for Work and Business

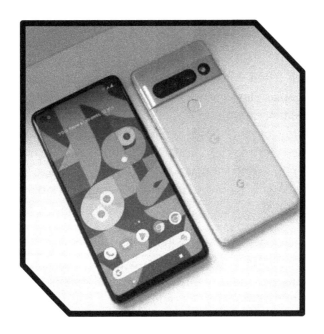

The Google Pixel 9 Pro is not just a high-end smartphone; it is also a powerful tool for business and professional use. Whether you need to manage emails, edit documents, attend virtual meetings, or collaborate with teams, this device offers seamless integration with cloud storage, office applications, and video conferencing platforms. Its AI-powered capabilities, advanced security features, and high-performance hardware make it an ideal companion for professionals, entrepreneurs, and remote workers. This chapter explores how to set up and optimize the Pixel 9 Pro for work-related tasks, ensuring maximum productivity, efficiency, and connectivity.

Setting Up Email and Cloud Storage

Email remains an essential tool for professional communication, and the Pixel 9 Pro supports all major email services, including Gmail, Microsoft Outlook, Yahoo Mail, and custom business email accounts. Setting up email accounts on the device is straightforward. Users can add their email accounts via the Settings app under Accounts > Add Account > Email. From there, selecting Gmail, Outlook, or any IMAP/POP3 provider allows seamless email synchronization.

For professionals who handle multiple email accounts, the Gmail app's unified inbox feature is invaluable, allowing users to view all emails in one place. Additionally, Google's AI-powered email categorization helps sort emails into Primary, Social, Promotions, and Updates, making it easier to focus on important messages while filtering out unnecessary notifications.

Cloud storage is another critical component for business users, enabling easy access to documents, presentations, spreadsheets, and multimedia files from anywhere. The Pixel 9 Pro seamlessly integrates with Google Drive, OneDrive, and Dropbox, ensuring users can store and retrieve files on the go. Setting up Google Drive is as simple as signing into a Google Account, and all files are automatically backed up, eliminating concerns about data loss. Business users can upload large files, share links with colleagues, and collaborate on documents in real-time, making cloud storage an essential productivity tool.

Using Microsoft Office and Google Workspace

For professionals who rely on document creation and management, the Pixel 9 Pro supports Microsoft Office and Google Workspace (formerly G Suite), ensuring that users can work on Word documents, Excel spreadsheets, and PowerPoint presentations directly from their device. Both Microsoft and Google provide fully functional mobile apps, enabling users to create, edit, and share documents without needing a laptop or desktop.

Microsoft Office apps, including Word, Excel, and PowerPoint, can be downloaded from the Google Play Store and linked to a Microsoft 365 account. These apps offer full compatibility with Windows and macOS versions, allowing users to work seamlessly across different devices. Features like track changes, cloud collaboration, and automatic backups ensure a smooth and productive workflow.

Google Workspace provides an equally powerful ecosystem, with Google Docs, Google Sheets, and Google Slides offering real-time collaboration. With Google Drive integration, team members can edit documents simultaneously, add comments, and track revisions effortlessly. The Pixel 9 Pro's advanced AI features, including voice-to-text and smart suggestions, further enhance productivity by allowing users to dictate notes, generate auto-complete suggestions, and quickly format documents.

Video Conferencing with Google Meet and Zoom

In today's professional world, virtual meetings and video conferencing are essential for collaboration. The Pixel 9 Pro's high-resolution front camera, powerful AI enhancements, and crystal-clear microphone make it one of the best smartphones for video calls. Whether using Google Meet, Zoom, Microsoft Teams, or Skype, the device ensures sharp video quality, noise cancellation, and stable connectivity.

Google Meet, which is deeply integrated with Google Workspace, allows users to host and join meetings effortlessly. Setting up a meeting is as simple as opening the Google Meet app, generating a link, and sharing it with participants. Google Meet offers AI-driven enhancements like real-time background blur, automatic lighting adjustments, and noise cancellation, ensuring a professional video call experience.

For businesses that rely on Zoom for client meetings and webinars, the Pixel 9 Pro provides a seamless Zoom experience. Users can schedule meetings, enable screen sharing, and record sessions directly from their device. Additionally, the Tensor G4 chip's AI-driven optimizations enhance video clarity, reduce lag, and optimize network bandwidth, ensuring that meetings run smoothly even in low connectivity environments.

Best Business Apps for Google Pixel

The Pixel 9 Pro's power and versatility make it an ideal device for running business applications. From task management and financial tracking to remote access and customer relationship management (CRM), the Play Store offers a wide range of apps tailored for business users.

1. Slack & Microsoft Teams – Essential for team collaboration, these apps enable real-time messaging, file sharing, and video conferencing.
2. Asana & Trello – Project management apps that help professionals track tasks, manage deadlines, and organize workflows efficiently.
3. Evernote & Google Keep – Perfect for taking notes, organizing ideas, and saving important documents on the go.
4. QuickBooks & FreshBooks – Useful for tracking expenses, generating invoices, and managing finances from a mobile device.

5. LastPass & Google Password Manager – Ensuring secure login management across multiple business accounts.
6. CamScanner & Adobe Scan – Allow users to scan documents, convert them into PDFs, and share them instantly.

For entrepreneurs and remote workers, the Pixel 9 Pro's AI-powered productivity tools, strong security features, and cloud-based ecosystem make it an indispensable device for managing business operations efficiently.

The Google Pixel 9 Pro is more than just a flagship smartphone—it is a powerful business tool designed to handle professional communication, document management, virtual meetings, and cloud storage seamlessly. By leveraging email integration, productivity apps, video conferencing tools, and advanced AI-driven enhancements, users can boost efficiency, streamline work processes, and stay connected no matter where they are. Whether you are a business executive, freelancer, entrepreneur, or remote worker, the Pixel 9 Pro provides all the tools necessary to manage work with ease and precision.

✻ Elara Technova

AI and Machine Learning on Pixel 9 Pro

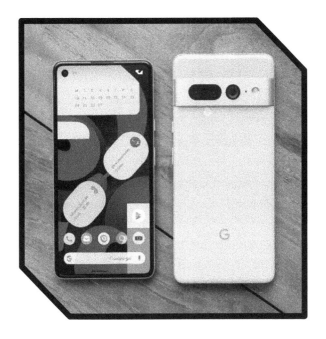

The Google Pixel 9 Pro is more than just a smartphone—it is a powerhouse of artificial intelligence (AI) and machine learning (ML), designed to make daily interactions smarter, faster, and more efficient. Google's commitment to on-device AI processing and cloud-based enhancements ensures that the Pixel 9 Pro offers intuitive experiences, real-time assistance, and personalized features. This chapter explores how AI enhances productivity, security, photography, and communication, while also looking at future AI advancements that will further improve the user experience.

Understanding On-Device AI Processing

One of the standout features of the Pixel 9 Pro is its Tensor G4 chip, which is optimized for AI-driven performance. Unlike many smartphones that rely heavily on cloud-based AI, the Pixel 9 Pro performs many AI calculations directly on the device. This results in faster processing, enhanced security, and reduced dependence on internet connectivity.

The Tensor G4's neural processing unit (NPU) is specifically designed to handle machine learning tasks efficiently. This allows the phone to learn user behaviors, optimize power consumption, improve app responsiveness, and enhance system-wide performance without needing external servers. On-device AI also improves privacy, as sensitive data like voice commands, facial recognition, and predictive text can be processed without being sent to the cloud.

Furthermore, adaptive learning allows the Pixel 9 Pro to adjust to your usage patterns over time. For example, the device prioritizes frequently used apps, predicts which apps you will open next, and optimizes battery usage based on your daily routine. These AI-driven enhancements make the device smarter and more efficient, ensuring a seamless and responsive user experience.

How Google AI Improves Everyday Tasks

AI is deeply integrated into almost every aspect of the Pixel 9 Pro, making everyday tasks faster, simpler, and more intuitive. The phone automatically enhances photos, translates languages in real-time, filters spam calls, and even summarizes text using AI-generated content suggestions.

For messaging, Smart Reply allows users to send quick, AI-generated responses without typing. This feature works across multiple apps, including Google Messages, WhatsApp, and Gmail, and adapts to your writing style. Additionally, Live Translate enables real-time language translation during conversations, making it an excellent tool for travelers or multilingual users.

The Pixel 9 Pro's AI-powered text recognition helps users extract text from images, scan documents, and convert handwritten notes into digital text instantly. This is particularly useful for students, professionals, and businesses that need to digitize documents quickly and accurately.

Another major AI-driven feature is Google Recorder, which transcribes audio recordings in real-time with near-perfect accuracy. Unlike traditional voice recorders, this feature can identify different speakers, highlight important points, and even generate summaries. This is particularly useful for journalists, students, and business professionals who frequently attend meetings or lectures.

Voice Recognition and AI-Powered Call Features

The Google Pixel 9 Pro boasts one of the most advanced voice recognition systems available on a smartphone. With Google Assistant deeply integrated into the system, voice commands are more accurate, faster, and highly personalized.

The phone's speech-to-text conversion is incredibly precise, allowing users to compose emails, send messages, take notes, and search the web entirely hands-free. Google's AI continuously learns your voice patterns, accents, and speaking style, making it even more responsive and accurate over time.

One of the most practical AI-driven features is Call Screen, which automatically answers unknown calls, detects spam, and even transcribes calls in real-time. If an incoming call is from an unknown number, Google Assistant will answer on your behalf, ask the caller for more details, and display a live transcript so you can decide whether to take the call. This helps users avoid spam, telemarketers, and robocalls.

Another impressive AI-powered tool is Hold for Me, which prevents users from waiting on hold for customer service calls. If you call a business and are placed on hold, the Pixel 9 Pro will wait for you and notify you when a live representative is available. This saves time and frustration, making long wait times a thing of the past.

Additionally, Clear Calling uses AI noise reduction to filter out background noise during calls, ensuring crystal-clear voice quality even in noisy environments. Whether you're on a busy street, in a crowded café, or at an airport, AI helps enhance your voice while reducing distractions from your surroundings.

Future AI Developments for Google Pixel

Google is continuously improving AI and machine learning technologies, and future updates for the

Pixel 9 Pro are expected to bring even more powerful AI-driven features. Google's Gemini AI, which is already enhancing search capabilities, is expected to be integrated more deeply into future Pixel updates, enabling advanced AI-driven conversations, better contextual understanding, and improved assistance for daily tasks.

One exciting future development is AI-powered predictive text summarization, which will allow Google Assistant to summarize long articles, emails, and documents in just a few seconds. This will be beneficial for professionals who need to quickly grasp key points without reading entire documents.

Another anticipated AI feature is Personalized AI Suggestions, which will analyze your habits, frequently used apps, and common activities to recommend the most relevant actions and shortcuts in real-time. This means your Pixel 9 Pro will be able to proactively suggest opening navigation when you get in your car, remind you of upcoming deadlines, and even suggest automated responses based on the context of your conversations.

Additionally, Google is working on more advanced AI-driven photography enhancements. Future updates are expected to include real-time object recognition, auto-enhanced video stabilization, and intelligent scene recommendations. This will allow users to capture professional-quality photos and videos effortlessly, without needing manual adjustments.

Google is also investing in AI-driven privacy enhancements, including on-device encryption, better facial recognition algorithms, and advanced malware protection. These improvements will ensure that users' data remains secure while still benefiting from the convenience of AI-powered tools.

The Google Pixel 9 Pro's AI and machine learning capabilities make it one of the smartest smartphones ever released. From enhanced photography and real-time transcription to intelligent call management and predictive text suggestions, AI improves nearly every aspect of the user experience. With on-device processing ensuring faster response times and enhanced privacy, the Pixel 9 Pro is a powerful tool for productivity, communication, and everyday convenience.

As Google continues to push the boundaries of AI and machine learning, future updates will only make the Pixel 9 Pro smarter, more intuitive, and even more efficient. Whether you are a business professional, student, traveler, or tech enthusiast, the AI-driven features of the Pixel 9 Pro offer unmatched convenience, efficiency, and performance.

Social Media and Content Creation

The Google Pixel 9 Pro is not just a smartphone; it is a powerful tool for content creators, social media influencers, and anyone who loves sharing their moments online. With its AI-powered camera system, intelligent photo and video editing tools, and seamless integration with popular social media platforms, the Pixel 9 Pro makes content creation easier and more professional than ever before. Whether you are capturing high-resolution images, shooting stunning 4K videos, or applying AI-enhanced filters, this chapter will guide you through the best settings, tools, and techniques to make your social media content stand out.

Best Camera Settings for Social Media

When it comes to creating high-quality social media content, using the right camera settings is crucial. The Pixel 9 Pro's triple-lens camera system, powered by Google's advanced AI, ensures that users can capture stunning, professional-quality images and videos with minimal effort.

For Instagram and TikTok, shooting in 4K resolution at 30 or 60 frames per second (fps) ensures that your videos are crisp, smooth, and visually appealing. The Super Res Zoom feature allows users to capture clear, detailed close-ups without losing quality, making it ideal for fashion, food, and travel photography. For those who enjoy selfies and vlogging, the ultra-wide front camera captures more background details while maintaining sharp focus on the subject.

The Portrait Mode is perfect for highlighting subjects while blurring the background, creating a professional, DSLR-like effect. This is ideal for profile pictures, beauty content, and lifestyle photography. Meanwhile, the Night Sight mode allows users to take bright and detailed photos even in low-light conditions, ensuring that night-time social media posts remain vivid and engaging.

Another important setting is HDR+ Enhanced, which balances shadows, highlights, and mid-tones to ensure that colors are natural and true-to-life. Whether you're photographing landscapes, portraits, or everyday moments, enabling HDR+ will enhance clarity, vibrancy, and detail, making your images more visually appealing for social media audiences.

Editing Photos and Videos for Instagram and TikTok

Once you've captured high-quality images and videos, the next step is editing them to perfection. The Pixel 9 Pro comes with Google's built-in AI-powered editing tools, including Magic Editor, Photo Unblur, and Video Boost, which make professional-level enhancements easy for anyone.

The Magic Editor allows users to effortlessly remove unwanted objects, adjust lighting, and reposition subjects within the frame, making it a game-changer for social media content creators. If you've taken a group photo but someone is slightly out of position, Magic Editor can shift them for a more balanced composition. It also lets users change the sky color, remove background distractions, and apply cinematic effects with a single tap.

For those who enjoy video content, the Pixel 9 Pro offers AI-powered video stabilization, ensuring that footage remains smooth even when filming on the go. The Super Slow-Motion mode captures high-speed action with stunning clarity, making it perfect for sports, dance videos, and creative transitions on TikTok.

Editing apps such as Snapseed, Adobe Lightroom, and Google Photos integrate seamlessly with Pixel's AI-powered tools, allowing users to adjust exposure, saturation, contrast, and sharpness for a polished look. Filters and presets can be applied to maintain a consistent aesthetic across all social media posts, ensuring that content remains visually appealing and professionally edited.

Using AI Filters and Enhancements

The Pixel 9 Pro's AI technology takes content creation to the next level by automatically applying intelligent enhancements to images and videos. With features like Face Unblur, Real Tone, and AI-enhanced beautification, the Pixel 9 Pro ensures that every shot looks its best.

Face Unblur sharpens faces in motion-heavy shots, making it ideal for action photography, event coverage, and spontaneous social media moments. This means that even if your subject moves suddenly, AI will correct any blurriness and maintain sharp details.

The Real Tone feature, exclusive to Google Pixel devices, ensures that skin tones appear natural and accurately represent all complexions. Unlike many smartphones that overcorrect or distort natural hues, Real Tone maintains authentic color representation, making it a powerful tool for diverse content creators.

For those who love using fun and engaging filters, the Pixel 9 Pro supports AI-powered filters in real-time, allowing users to preview and apply dynamic effects before capturing an image or video. Whether you prefer vintage aesthetics, cinematic looks, or high-contrast edits, these filters enhance visual appeal without requiring third-party apps.

Additionally, Google's AI beautification tools allow subtle refinements like smoothing skin, whitening teeth, and reducing glare while keeping the natural texture and authenticity of the subject. This ensures that users can create flawless yet realistic social media content with ease.

Scheduling and Managing Social Media Posts

Creating great content is just one part of social media success—timing and consistency are equally important. The Pixel 9 Pro offers powerful tools for managing and scheduling posts to ensure that content reaches the right audience at the right time.

Using Google Assistant, users can set reminders to post at peak engagement times, ensuring that content gets maximum visibility and interaction. The Google Calendar integration allows creators to plan and organize content schedules, making it easier to maintain a consistent posting strategy.

For businesses and influencers, apps like Meta Business Suite, Hootsuite, and Buffer work seamlessly with the Pixel 9 Pro, enabling users to schedule posts, analyze performance metrics, and engage with followers across multiple platforms. These apps provide real-time analytics on which posts are performing well, helping users adjust their strategy for better engagement.

The Pixel 9 Pro's AI-generated captions feature helps content creators come up with engaging and relevant descriptions for posts, ensuring that they include hashtags, keywords, and trending topics for maximum reach. Additionally, Google's voice-to-text feature allows users to dictate captions effortlessly, making content creation faster and more efficient.

Another useful feature is social media automation, where Google Assistant can help auto-reply to comments, send pre-written responses, and engage with followers in real-time. This is especially beneficial for businesses, influencers, and brands looking to maintain an active online presence without spending hours managing interactions manually.

The Google Pixel 9 Pro is one of the best smartphones for social media content creation, offering AI-powered photography tools, advanced video editing features, and seamless social media integration. With high-quality camera settings, intelligent filters, and automated posting tools, users can capture, edit, and share stunning content with ease.

Whether you're a professional content creator, an influencer, or someone who simply loves sharing life's moments, the Pixel 9 Pro's cutting-edge AI and intuitive editing features make it the ultimate device for modern social media storytelling.

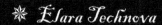

Health and Fitness Tracking

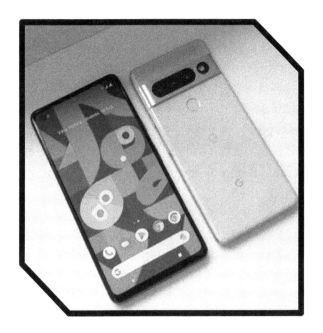

The Google Pixel 9 Pro is more than just a smartphone—it is a powerful health and fitness companion designed to help users track their physical activities, monitor sleep patterns, and improve overall well-being. With advanced sensors, AI-powered fitness tracking, and seamless integration with wearables, the Pixel 9 Pro makes it easy for users to maintain a healthy lifestyle. Whether you are looking to track workouts, monitor heart rate, or manage stress levels, this chapter provides a comprehensive guide to using the Pixel 9 Pro as your ultimate fitness and health assistant.

Using Google Fit for Activity Tracking

Google Fit is the primary health and fitness app for Android users, providing a centralized platform to monitor daily activity, exercise routines, and overall fitness progress. With the Pixel 9 Pro's built-in motion sensors, Google Fit automatically detects walking, running, cycling, and other exercises, ensuring that every movement is accurately recorded.

One of the standout features of Google Fit is its Heart Points and Move Minutes system, which encourages users to stay active by rewarding points for movement and exercise. The app tracks steps, calories burned, and distance traveled, giving users a clear picture of their daily physical activity. Whether you are going for a jog, hiking, or simply taking a brisk walk, Google Fit ensures that every step counts.

Users can also set custom fitness goals based on daily activity levels, weight management, or endurance training. With AI-powered insights,

Google Fit provides personalized recommendations to help users stay motivated and achieve their fitness targets. The Pixel 9 Pro's AI processing also enables automatic workout detection, making it easier than ever to log exercise sessions without manually entering data.

For users who prefer a more detailed breakdown of their health statistics, Google Fit offers integration with third-party apps like Strava, MyFitnessPal, and Fitbit, allowing data to be synced across multiple platforms for a more holistic view of overall wellness.

Connecting Wearables and Fitness Bands

The Google Pixel 9 Pro is designed to seamlessly connect with a wide range of smartwatches, fitness bands, and health monitoring devices, enhancing real-time tracking of fitness metrics. Whether using a Google Pixel Watch, Fitbit, or other Wear OS-powered wearables, the Pixel 9 Pro provides fast and reliable synchronization to ensure that health data remains accurate and up to date.

For users with a Pixel Watch or Fitbit, real-time heart rate monitoring, sleep tracking, and stress detection are automatically recorded and displayed on both the wearable and the Google Fit app. These insights help users understand their fitness trends and make data-driven decisions about exercise routines, diet, and recovery periods.

Pairing a fitness band or smartwatch with the Pixel 9 Pro allows for hands-free control of workout tracking, music playback, and notifications during exercise. Users can also set up automatic workout reminders, ensuring that they stay consistent with their fitness goals. Additionally, wearables provide live coaching feedback, helping users improve their form, optimize workout intensity, and reduce the risk of injury.

Google's Fast Pair technology ensures that connecting a smartwatch or fitness tracker to the Pixel 9 Pro is quick and hassle-free. With one-tap pairing, users can instantly sync their devices, allowing for a seamless and uninterrupted fitness tracking experience.

Best Workout and Meditation Apps

The Pixel 9 Pro supports a variety of workout, meditation, and mental wellness apps, making it a versatile tool for both physical and mental health. Whether you prefer guided workouts, strength training, yoga, or meditation sessions, there are several top-rated apps that integrate seamlessly with the Google Fit ecosystem.

For users looking to build muscle, improve endurance, or lose weight, apps like Nike Training Club, Adidas Runtastic, and MyFitnessPal provide personalized workout plans, real-time coaching, and performance tracking. These apps also sync with Google Fit, ensuring that all exercise data is consolidated in one place for easy monitoring.

Yoga and flexibility training enthusiasts can benefit from apps like Down Dog, Yoga for Beginners, and Daily Yoga, which offer step-by-step guidance, voice instructions, and AI-powered pose corrections to help users improve balance, flexibility, and core strength.

For mental wellness, meditation apps like Headspace, Calm, and Insight Timer provide guided breathing exercises, mindfulness techniques, and sleep stories that promote relaxation and stress relief. The Pixel 9 Pro's built-in AI assistant can also be used to set meditation reminders, play calming background sounds, and guide users through breathing exercises for better mental clarity and relaxation.

Using Pixel 9 Pro for Sleep Tracking

A good night's sleep is essential for overall health, and the Google Pixel 9 Pro provides advanced tools for monitoring and improving sleep patterns.

Whether you have trouble falling asleep, staying asleep, or waking up feeling refreshed, the Pixel 9 Pro offers AI-powered insights to help optimize your sleep cycle.

For users with a Google Pixel Watch or a compatible wearable, sleep tracking is automatically recorded and displayed in Google Fit. The device monitors sleep duration, movement, breathing patterns, and heart rate variability, providing a detailed breakdown of sleep quality. Users can also set smart alarms that wake them up at the optimal time based on their natural sleep cycles, helping them feel more refreshed and energized in the morning.

The Bedtime Mode feature on the Pixel 9 Pro helps users reduce screen time before bed by enabling greyscale mode, limiting notifications, and reducing blue light exposure, which can interfere with melatonin production. Users can schedule Bedtime Mode through Google's Digital Wellbeing settings, ensuring that their phone automatically switches to a sleep-friendly mode at night.

Additionally, the Pixel 9 Pro's AI-powered sleep sounds feature allows users to play white noise, nature sounds, or calming music to create a soothing sleep environment. Integrations with apps like Calm and Sleep Cycle also provide sleep tracking data, relaxation techniques, and bedtime stories to improve restfulness and relaxation.

For users who experience irregular sleep patterns, the Pixel 9 Pro's AI-powered insights analyze sleep trends over time and provide recommendations to improve sleep hygiene. Whether it's adjusting bedtime, limiting screen exposure, or improving sleep posture, the Pixel 9 Pro helps users take control of their sleep health.

The Google Pixel 9 Pro is an all-in-one health and fitness companion, providing users with powerful tools for tracking workouts, monitoring sleep, and improving overall well-being. With seamless integration with Google Fit, advanced AI-powered fitness tracking, and compatibility with a range of wearables, users can stay on top of their health goals with ease.

Whether you are a fitness enthusiast, a casual exerciser, or someone looking to improve sleep and mental well-being, the Pixel 9 Pro offers intelligent and user-friendly features to help you lead a healthier and more balanced lifestyle.

Photography for Beginners and Professionals

The Google Pixel 9 Pro is equipped with a high-end camera system designed to provide exceptional photography experiences for both beginners and professional photographers. With AI-powered enhancements, advanced HDR capabilities, and support for RAW photography, the Pixel 9 Pro's camera system is one of the best in the smartphone industry. Whether you want to capture stunning landscapes, take professional-quality portraits, or edit images like a pro, this chapter will guide you through the best features and techniques to master photography on the Pixel 9 Pro.

Mastering Portrait Mode and AI Enhancements

Portrait photography has become one of the most widely used camera features, and the Pixel 9 Pro takes it to the next level with AI-powered depth sensing, background blur adjustments, and subject detection. The advanced portrait mode ensures that subjects are captured with sharp details and beautiful background separation, making images appear professional and polished.

One of the standout features of the Pixel 9 Pro's portrait mode is its ability to adjust the depth of field after taking a photo. This means users can fine-tune the blur intensity to create a bokeh effect similar to DSLR cameras. The AI enhancements also help improve skin tones, remove blemishes, and enhance facial details naturally, without making the subject look overly edited.

For group shots or capturing moving subjects, the Face Unblur tool ensures that every face remains sharp and in focus, even in challenging conditions.

The Magic Eraser feature allows users to remove unwanted objects or people from the background, creating a clean and distraction-free composition.

Low-light portrait photography is also greatly improved with Night Sight in Portrait Mode, which uses AI-driven image stacking and noise reduction to produce bright and detailed photos in dark environments. This feature is particularly useful for evening gatherings, indoor portraits, or nighttime cityscapes, where traditional cameras may struggle to capture details.

Shooting HDR and RAW Photos

High Dynamic Range (HDR) photography is essential for capturing images with rich details, accurate colors, and balanced exposure levels. The Pixel 9 Pro utilizes HDR+ technology to combine multiple exposures into a single, well-balanced image, preventing overexposed highlights or underexposed shadows.

HDR+ is particularly useful for scenes with high contrast, such as sunsets, bright cityscapes, and backlit subjects. The Pixel 9 Pro's AI processing ensures that each HDR image is optimized for natural color reproduction and depth, making images look realistic and immersive.

For professional photographers who want greater control over editing, the Pixel 9 Pro supports RAW photography. Shooting in RAW format preserves all the image data from the camera sensor, allowing for advanced post-processing adjustments in apps like Adobe Lightroom, Snapseed, or Photoshop. Users can adjust exposure, color grading, and sharpness without losing quality, making RAW photography ideal for professional edits and print-quality images.

To enable RAW capture, users need to turn on RAW + JPEG mode in the camera settings. This allows them to capture both a high-quality processed JPEG and an uncompressed RAW file for maximum editing flexibility.

Editing Photos with Google Photos and Third-Party Apps

After capturing a photo, editing plays a crucial role in enhancing its quality. The Pixel 9 Pro comes with built-in AI-powered editing tools in Google Photos, allowing users to adjust brightness, contrast, saturation, and sharpness with ease. The Magic Editor feature lets users reposition objects, adjust lighting conditions, and enhance details effortlessly.

For quick and easy edits, Google Photos provides AI-powered suggestions, including Auto Enhance, Color Pop, and Skin Tone Adjustments, which instantly improve images with one tap. The HDR effect can also be applied to older photos, adding depth and detail to previously captured images.

For those who prefer more advanced editing capabilities, third-party apps like Adobe Lightroom, VSCO, and Snapseed offer powerful tools for professional-grade edits. These apps allow users to apply filters, fine-tune exposure, sharpen details, and create unique artistic effects. The Pixel 9 Pro's high-resolution camera ensures that edited photos maintain their quality even after extensive modifications.

Editing also extends to video enhancement, where apps like CapCut, Adobe Premiere Rush, and KineMaster can be used to trim clips, add music, and apply cinematic filters. The Pixel 9 Pro's AI stabilization and 4K recording capabilities make it an excellent device for capturing and editing high-quality video content directly from the phone.

Best Photography Accessories for Pixel 9 Pro

To maximize the photography potential of the Pixel 9 Pro, users can invest in a variety of accessories that enhance stability, lighting, and creativity.

- Tripods and Gimbals: A compact tripod or a motorized gimbal is essential for steady shots, long-exposure photography, and time-lapse videos. Popular choices include DJI Osmo Mobile, Joby GorillaPod, and Zhiyun Smooth gimbals, which provide stable shooting conditions for both photos and videos.

- Clip-On Lenses: While the Pixel 9 Pro has a powerful built-in camera, adding clip-on lenses such as wide-angle, macro, or fisheye lenses can provide creative perspectives and unique effects.
- Portable LED Lights: For night photography and low-light conditions, a small LED light panel or ring light can significantly improve brightness and color accuracy. Devices like Lume Cube or Aputure LED panels provide adjustable lighting for professional-quality images.
- Wireless Shutter Remotes: A Bluetooth remote shutter allows users to capture photos without touching the phone, making it ideal for group shots, long-exposure shots, and hands-free photography.
- Waterproof Cases: For users who love underwater photography, a waterproof phone case or diving housing can allow them to capture stunning ocean, pool, or rain shots without damaging the device.

The Google Pixel 9 Pro's camera system is one of the most advanced in the industry, offering AI-enhanced photography, professional editing tools, and versatile shooting modes. Whether you are a beginner learning the basics of portrait photography or a professional seeking RAW image control, the Pixel 9 Pro delivers an exceptional photography experience. With powerful software enhancements, seamless Google Photos integration, and a range of useful accessories, this device allows users to capture and edit breathtaking photos with ease.

※ *Elara Technova*

Audio and Sound Features

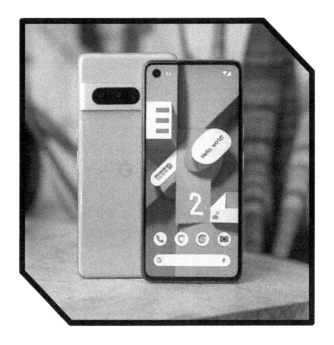

The Google Pixel 9 Pro is equipped with high-quality stereo speakers, advanced audio processing, and seamless connectivity with wireless audio devices, making it an excellent choice for music lovers, podcast listeners, and those who enjoy an immersive audio experience. This chapter will explore the Pixel 9 Pro's sound capabilities, customization settings, and best practices for optimizing audio quality. Whether you're streaming music, making crystal-clear calls, or fine-tuning sound preferences, understanding how to make the most of your device's audio features will enhance your overall experience.

Understanding Stereo Speakers and Spatial Audio

The Google Pixel 9 Pro features dual stereo speakers that deliver clear, loud, and well-balanced sound. Unlike single-speaker setups found in some smartphones, the stereo speakers on the Pixel 9 Pro create an immersive audio experience that enhances both music playback and video streaming. The sound output is tuned for clarity, depth, and spatial awareness, making it ideal for enjoying movies, podcasts, and games without external speakers or headphones.

One of the standout audio features of the Pixel 9 Pro is Spatial Audio, which creates a 3D-like sound effect for a more engaging listening experience. When using compatible headphones or earbuds, Spatial Audio adjusts the sound based on head movements, making the audio feel more realistic and immersive. This feature is particularly useful for gaming, virtual reality experiences, and high-quality movie streaming, as it gives the impression that the sound is coming from different directions rather than from a single source.

In addition to Spatial Audio, the Adaptive Sound feature allows the Pixel 9 Pro to automatically adjust speaker volume and audio output based on the environmental noise levels. If you are in a quiet room, the device will fine-tune the sound to be softer and more balanced, whereas in a noisy environment, it will enhance the audio to make it clearer and louder. This ensures that you always get the best sound quality without constantly adjusting the volume manually.

Best Music and Podcast Apps for Google Pixel

With powerful audio features, the Pixel 9 Pro is an excellent device for streaming music and listening to podcasts. There are numerous apps available for high-quality audio streaming, offline listening, and personalized recommendations.

For music streaming, apps like Spotify, YouTube Music, and Apple Music offer millions of songs, curated playlists, and high-fidelity audio. Spotify Premium provides lossless audio and AI-generated playlists based on your listening habits, while YouTube Music integrates seamlessly with Google Assistant for voice commands and personalized recommendations. Apple Music's lossless audio feature ensures studio-quality sound for audiophiles.

For podcast lovers, apps like Google Podcasts, Pocket Casts, and Audible offer a wide selection of content across different genres, including news, entertainment, education, and self-improvement. Google Podcasts syncs across all Google devices, allowing users to continue listening from where they left off. Audible provides audiobooks with professional narrations, perfect for those who prefer listening to books rather than reading them.

Users who prefer local music playback can use Poweramp or VLC Media Player, which support various file formats such as MP3, FLAC, and WAV, offering equalizer settings to enhance sound quality.

Connecting Wireless Headphones and Audio Devices

The Pixel 9 Pro is designed to work seamlessly with a variety of wireless audio devices, including Bluetooth headphones, earbuds, and external speakers. The device supports Bluetooth 5.3, which provides faster connection speeds, improved range, and lower latency for an uninterrupted audio experience.

To connect a Bluetooth device, simply go to:

- Settings > Connected Devices > Bluetooth > Pair New Device
- Ensure your Bluetooth headphones or speakers are in pairing mode
- Select the device from the list and tap Pair

The Fast Pair feature on the Pixel 9 Pro allows quick and easy pairing with supported earbuds like Google Pixel Buds, Bose QuietComfort, or Sony WH-1000XM series. Fast Pair also syncs your Bluetooth devices across all Google accounts, so you don't need to reconnect when switching between devices like a Pixel tablet or Chromebook.

For wired audio connections, the Pixel 9 Pro supports USB-C headphones and DAC (Digital-to-Analog Converter) adapters, ensuring high-resolution sound quality. USB-C headphones like the Google Pixel USB-C Earbuds or Sennheiser Momentum deliver premium sound quality with built-in microphones for calls and voice commands.

The device also supports multi-device audio switching, which allows seamless transitions between multiple Bluetooth devices. For example, if you are listening to music on your wireless earbuds and receive a call on your Pixel 9 Pro, the audio will automatically switch from music playback to the call, and then back to music once the call ends.

For those who use smart home speakers like Google Nest Audio or Sonos, the Pixel 9 Pro allows casting music and podcasts wirelessly via Google Cast. This means users can start playing audio on their phone and continue listening through external speakers with just a single tap.

Customizing Audio Settings for Calls and Media

The Pixel 9 Pro includes various audio settings that enhance the sound experience for both calls and media playback. Users can adjust equalizer settings, enable noise cancellation, and configure call audio preferences for a personalized experience.

The Adaptive Sound setting, available in Settings > Sound & Vibration, automatically adjusts the volume and clarity of audio depending on the surroundings. This feature is useful for those who take phone calls in different environments, ensuring that voices remain clear and understandable.

For music and media, users can customize bass, treble, and balance levels by accessing the Equalizer settings in their preferred music or podcast app. This feature allows users to fine-tune the audio to match their personal preference, whether they enjoy deep bass, crisp highs, or balanced sound.

The Live Caption feature enhances accessibility by automatically generating captions for any audio content playing on the phone, making it easier to understand spoken words in videos, podcasts, or voice messages.

For call quality, the Pixel 9 Pro includes Noise Suppression and Clear Calling, which reduce background noise and enhance voice clarity during calls. These features ensure that both parties can hear each other clearly, even in noisy environments like busy streets, crowded cafés, or public transport.

Users can also take advantage of the Call Screening feature, which allows Google Assistant to filter spam calls and provide real-time transcripts before deciding whether to answer the call. This helps eliminate unwanted calls while ensuring important calls are answered promptly.

The Google Pixel 9 Pro offers an advanced and customizable audio experience, with stereo speakers, spatial audio, and seamless Bluetooth connectivity. Whether you are a music enthusiast, podcast listener, or someone who frequently takes calls on the go, the Pixel 9 Pro delivers crisp, immersive, and adaptive sound quality. With customizable audio settings, wireless audio support, and intelligent AI-powered enhancements, this device ensures that every sound, song, and conversation is crystal clear and optimized for user comfort.

Traveling with Google Pixel 9 Pro

The Google Pixel 9 Pro is an excellent companion for travelers, offering powerful navigation tools, offline accessibility, high-quality photography, and seamless global connectivity. Whether you're exploring a new city, driving cross-country, or traveling internationally, this device is designed to keep you connected, informed, and prepared. With features like Google

Maps, offline access, AI-powered translation, and advanced camera technology, the Pixel 9 Pro enhances every aspect of travel, making it easier to navigate, communicate, and capture stunning memories.

Using Google Maps and GPS Navigation

One of the most essential tools for any traveler is Google Maps, and the Pixel 9 Pro takes full advantage of its AI-driven navigation and real-time updates. Whether you are walking, driving, cycling, or using public transport, Google Maps provides detailed directions, estimated arrival times, and live traffic updates to help you plan your journey efficiently.

When using Google Maps for driving, the Pixel 9 Pro's high-precision GPS and real-time traffic monitoring ensure that you take the fastest and most efficient route. The app provides turn-by-turn navigation, voice guidance, and alternative routes if traffic conditions change. Live traffic alerts warn you about accidents, road closures, and delays, allowing you to avoid congestion and reach your destination faster.

For those who prefer walking or cycling, Google Maps offers step-by-step directions with augmented reality (AR). This feature overlays navigation instructions directly onto real-world views using the Pixel 9 Pro's camera, making it easier to follow routes in unfamiliar places.

Public transportation users can benefit from real-time bus, train, and metro schedules, including arrival predictions and service updates. The Pixel 9 Pro ensures that you are always aware of changes in transit schedules, delays, and alternate routes to reach your destination without confusion.

Downloading Offline Maps and Translation Apps

One of the biggest challenges while traveling is navigating in areas with limited or no internet access. Thankfully, the Pixel 9 Pro allows you to download offline maps, ensuring that you can navigate even when you're disconnected. To do this:

- Open Google Maps
- Search for the city or region you'll be visiting
- Tap on the "Download" button to save an offline version of the map

With offline maps, you can search for locations, get directions, and view points of interest without using mobile data. This is particularly useful for international travel, where data roaming charges can be expensive.

Another essential tool for travelers is Google Translate, which is integrated into the Pixel 9 Pro. This app helps you communicate in different languages by translating text, speech, and images in real time. The Live Translate feature allows you to point your camera at signs, menus, or written text and get an instant translation. Additionally, conversation mode enables real-time spoken translations, making it easier to interact with locals and navigate foreign environments.

For offline translation, you can download language packs in Google Translate, ensuring that you can translate phrases and text even without an internet connection. This is extremely helpful when visiting countries where English is not widely spoken.

International Roaming and eSIM Setup

Staying connected while traveling internationally is crucial for communication, navigation, and emergency situations. The Pixel 9 Pro supports eSIM technology, allowing users to activate a local data plan without needing a physical SIM card. This is particularly useful for frequent travelers who want to avoid expensive roaming fees and switch between carriers seamlessly.

Setting up an eSIM on the Pixel 9 Pro is simple:

- Open Settings > Network & Internet
- Select Mobile Network and tap Add eSIM
- Scan a QR code from a supported carrier or choose an available provider
- Follow the instructions to activate your new mobile plan

Many international carriers and travel SIM providers now offer prepaid eSIM plans, allowing you to activate a local mobile network before arriving at your destination. This eliminates the hassle of purchasing a SIM card upon arrival and provides instant access to mobile data, calls, and texts.

For those who prefer traditional SIM cards, the Pixel 9 Pro's dual SIM functionality allows you to use both a physical SIM and an eSIM simultaneously, making it easier to switch between networks based on coverage and pricing.

Additionally, Google Fi, a network designed for international travelers, works seamlessly on the Pixel 9 Pro, offering affordable global data plans across 200+ countries. If your carrier does not provide affordable roaming, using Google Fi or a travel SIM can save you significant costs on data and calls while abroad.

One of the most exciting aspects of travel is capturing unforgettable moments, and the Pixel 9 Pro's advanced camera system makes it the perfect travel photography companion. Whether you're photographing landscapes, cityscapes, or cultural experiences, the device's AI-powered camera features ensure that every shot looks professional and high-quality.

For scenic photography, using Night Sight and HDR+ modes enhances details in low-light conditions and bright outdoor settings. The Pixel 9 Pro's Ultra-Wide Lens is perfect for capturing expansive landscapes, while the Telephoto Lens allows you to zoom in on distant objects without losing quality.

If you're capturing portraits or street photography, the Magic Editor and Face Unblur tools help you remove distractions and enhance facial details, making images look more refined and polished.

For travel vlogging, the Pixel 9 Pro's 4K video recording with AI stabilization ensures that your videos remain smooth and cinematic. Whether you're walking through bustling markets or capturing breathtaking aerial views, the camera's advanced stabilization technology eliminates shakiness, resulting in professional-looking footage.

Another great feature for travelers is Live Translate for captions and subtitles, which can instantly translate spoken words into text in different languages. This is useful for interviewing locals, recording guided tours, or documenting travel experiences in multiple languages.

To protect your travel photos and videos, using Google Photos' automatic backup feature ensures that your memories are safely stored in the cloud. This allows you to free up space on your device while having access to all your travel shots anytime, anywhere.

The Google Pixel 9 Pro is a powerful and reliable travel companion, designed to enhance your journeys with seamless navigation, smart translation tools, high-quality photography, and worldwide connectivity. Whether you're exploring a new city, embarking on an international adventure, or simply commuting in a foreign country, this device provides all the tools you need to travel smarter and more efficiently. With offline access, AI-powered photography, and flexible connectivity options, the Pixel 9 Pro ensures that you stay connected, informed, and ready to capture every memorable moment.

Advanced Android Features

The Google Pixel 9 Pro comes with a variety of advanced features that allow users to unlock deeper customization, enhance security, automate daily tasks, and take full control of their device's capabilities. With Android 15, Google has introduced improved developer tools, smarter privacy controls, and AI-driven automation, making it easier to personalize your experience while maintaining performance and security. This chapter will guide you through unlocking developer mode, managing app permissions, using Google Assistant for task automation, and exploring hidden Android 15 features that can improve efficiency and enhance user experience.

Unlocking Developer Mode and Debugging Tools

Android devices come with a hidden Developer Mode that allows users to access advanced system settings, enable debugging options, and optimize device performance. The Google Pixel 9 Pro has a range of developer options that can enhance speed, tweak animations, and provide deeper control over the operating system.

To enable Developer Mode, follow these steps:

- Go to Settings > About Phone
- Scroll down and tap Build Number seven times
- You will see a message stating "You are now a developer!"

Once Developer Mode is enabled, you will gain access to powerful features such as USB debugging, animation speed controls, background process limits, and GPU rendering options. USB debugging is particularly useful for connecting your Pixel 9

Pro to a computer for troubleshooting, transferring files, or developing applications.

One useful feature within Developer Options is forcing peak refresh rate, which ensures that the Pixel 9 Pro's 120Hz display runs at its highest refresh rate at all times, making animations smoother and improving gaming performance. Another important option is background process limit, which allows users to restrict the number of background apps running to improve battery life and performance.

Additionally, users who are interested in customizing the Pixel 9 Pro can use OEM unlocking, which is a setting in Developer Mode that allows users to unlock the bootloader and install custom ROMs or third-party software. However, unlocking the bootloader disables some security features and can void the warranty, so it should be used with caution.

Understanding App Permissions and Privacy Settings

Privacy and security are top priorities for modern smartphone users, and the Pixel 9 Pro offers advanced app permission controls to help users protect their data. Android 15 introduces new privacy features that allow users to control what data each app can access, monitor permissions in real time, and revoke permissions for unused apps.

To manage app permissions, go to Settings > Privacy > Permission Manager. This section allows users to see which apps have access to location, camera, microphone, contacts, and storage. If an app has unnecessary access to sensitive data, you can easily revoke its permissions.

One of the most important security features in Android 15 is one-time permissions, which allows apps to access certain data only while they are in use. For example, if you grant a navigation app access to your location, it will only have access while the app is open. As soon as you close the app, the permission is automatically revoked.

Another key feature is privacy indicators, which alert users whenever an app is accessing the microphone, camera, or location. A small green dot will appear in the status bar to notify you when an app is using these features.

To further enhance privacy, users can enable Google Play Protect, which scans apps for malware and alerts users about potentially harmful software. This feature helps protect your Pixel 9 Pro from malicious apps that could compromise data or slow down performance.

Google Assistant on the Pixel 9 Pro is more than just a voice-activated assistant—it can automate daily tasks, set up personalized routines, and integrate with smart home devices. With Google Assistant Routines, users can trigger multiple actions with a single voice command, saving time and streamlining productivity.

To set up a routine, follow these steps:

- Open Google Assistant and go to Settings
- Tap Routines and choose "Create a new routine"
- Add a trigger phrase (e.g., "Good morning" or "Start my workout")
- Select the actions you want to automate (e.g., turn on Wi-Fi, read the weather, play music, send a text, or adjust smart home devices)

For example, if you create a morning routine, you can set it to:

- Turn off Do Not Disturb mode
- Read out calendar events and reminders
- Give a weather update
- Turn on smart lights
- Start playing a morning playlist on Spotify

Google Assistant Routines can also be location-based, meaning they will automatically trigger when you arrive at or leave a specific place. This is useful for tasks such as turning on home security cameras when leaving the house or enabling silent mode when arriving at work.

For fitness enthusiasts, Google Assistant can automate workout reminders, start a fitness tracker, and read out health statistics from Google Fit.

With AI-powered automation, the Pixel 9 Pro helps simplify daily routines, making it easier to focus on tasks without constantly adjusting settings manually.

Best Hidden Android 15 Features

Android 15 introduces several hidden features that enhance usability, customization, and security on the Pixel 9 Pro. These features are not always obvious, but they greatly improve the overall user experience.

One useful feature is Predictive Back Gesture, which allows users to see a preview of the screen they will return to when using the back gesture. This prevents accidental exits from apps and provides a smoother navigation experience.

Another hidden feature is Clipboard Privacy Protection, which ensures that copied content does not remain accessible indefinitely. Android 15 automatically clears clipboard data after a short period, preventing apps from reading sensitive information such as passwords or personal messages.

The "Lockdown Mode" feature is another hidden security tool that disables biometric authentication (face unlock and fingerprint) with a single tap, forcing the use of a PIN or password for unlocking. This is useful in situations where you need extra security, such as when traveling or leaving your phone unattended.

For gamers, Android 15 includes a Game Dashboard that allows users to optimize gaming performance, enable screen recording, and view real-time FPS (frames per second). This feature ensures a better gaming experience by balancing battery usage and performance.

Additionally, Live Captions now work in multiple languages and can generate instant subtitles for videos, voice messages, and phone calls, making communication more accessible for users with hearing impairments or language barriers.

Another powerful feature is App Archiving, which allows users to temporarily uninstall apps while keeping their data stored, freeing up space without losing important settings or preferences.

The Google Pixel 9 Pro with Android 15 is packed with powerful features, advanced security controls, and AI-driven automation tools. By unlocking Developer Mode, managing app permissions, automating routines with Google Assistant, and exploring hidden Android features, users can maximize the potential of their device. Whether you're a power user looking for advanced customization or someone who wants a more efficient and secure smartphone experience, these tools allow you to take full control over your Pixel 9 Pro.

Keeping Your Pixel Secure and Updated

Keeping your Google Pixel 9 Pro secure and updated is essential to ensuring its long-term functionality, protecting personal data, and preventing cyber threats. With Android 15, Google has introduced stronger security measures, real-time system updates, and enhanced privacy tools to keep users safe. This chapter provides a comprehensive guide on managing security patches, using VPNs for private browsing, configuring Google Play Protect, and securing personal and work data. By following these security measures, users can maintain the highest level of protection and privacy while using their device.

Managing Security Patches and OS Updates

Keeping your Pixel 9 Pro's software updated is one of the most important ways to stay protected from vulnerabilities, malware, and system exploits. Google regularly releases security patches, bug fixes, and OS updates that not only improve performance but also address newly discovered threats.

To check for and install software updates, follow these steps:

- Open Settings on your Pixel 9 Pro
- Scroll down to System
- Tap System update
- If an update is available, tap Download and Install

Android 15 introduces seamless background updates, which allow certain security patches to be installed in the background without interrupting your usage. Google's Play System Updates also provide smaller security fixes without requiring a full system reboot.

It is highly recommended to enable automatic updates so that your device always stays secure. To do this, go to Settings > System > System update > Auto-update system. When enabled, your Pixel 9 Pro will automatically download and install updates when connected to Wi-Fi, ensuring that your device is always protected against the latest security threats.

For users who prefer manual updates, it is advisable to check for updates at least once a month to ensure that your device remains up to date. Keeping your Pixel 9 Pro updated is critical for preventing hackers from exploiting system vulnerabilities, especially since Google frequently patches security flaws in their monthly security bulletins.

Using VPNs for Private Browsing

A Virtual Private Network (VPN) is an excellent tool for protecting your online privacy, encrypting your internet traffic, and securing your personal data from cyber threats. With increasing concerns over data privacy and tracking, using a VPN on your Pixel 9 Pro is a great way to prevent unauthorized access to your internet activity.

A VPN works by masking your IP address and encrypting your data, making it nearly impossible for hackers, advertisers, or government surveillance programs to track your online activities. This is especially useful when using public Wi-Fi networks, where security is often weak and susceptible to attacks.

To set up a VPN on your Pixel 9 Pro, follow these steps:

- Go to Settings > Network & internet > VPN
- Tap Add VPN and enter the required details from your VPN provider
- Alternatively, download a trusted VPN app from the Google Play Store
- Open the VPN app, sign in, and connect to a server of your choice

When selecting a VPN service, it's best to choose one that offers end-to-end encryption, a no-log policy, and a kill switch feature. Some of the best VPN providers for Google Pixel 9 Pro include NordVPN, ExpressVPN, and Surfshark, all of which offer high-speed connections, strong security protocols, and multiple server locations.

Using a VPN can also help you access region-locked content on streaming services and prevent Internet Service Providers (ISPs) from tracking your browsing habits. For users who travel frequently, a VPN ensures secure internet access from any location, making it an essential tool for data protection.

Configuring Google Play Protect

Google Play Protect is an advanced security system built into every Android device, including the Pixel 9 Pro. It helps protect your phone by scanning apps for malware, blocking harmful downloads, and providing real-time security updates.

To ensure Google Play Protect is enabled, follow these steps:

- Open Google Play Store
- Tap Menu (three horizontal lines) > Play Protect
- Ensure that "Scan apps with Play Protect" is turned on

Google Play Protect automatically scans apps installed on your device and alerts you if any suspicious activity is detected. It also monitors apps for unusual behavior, such as unauthorized access to personal data, high battery consumption, or suspicious background activity.

One of the best features of Google Play Protect is that it analyzes newly installed apps before they run, ensuring that no malicious software can harm your device. If Play Protect identifies a potentially harmful app, it will notify the user and provide the option to uninstall it immediately.

Additionally, Google Play Protect regularly updates its security database, meaning that your device will be protected against the latest malware and cyber threats. It is recommended to manually scan your device for security threats at least once a week by going to Google Play Store > Play Protect > Scan.

For users who sideload apps from third-party sources, Play Protect also helps detect unauthorized installations and warns users before allowing such apps to run. This is crucial for preventing malware infections from unverified sources.

Securing Personal and Work Data

Keeping personal and work data secure is more important than ever, especially with the growing risks of data breaches, phishing attacks, and identity theft. The Pixel 9 Pro provides multiple layers of security, allowing users to protect their files, photos, and sensitive information from unauthorized access.

One of the most effective ways to secure personal data is by using biometric authentication, such as Face Unlock and Fingerprint Scanner. These features add an extra layer of protection, ensuring that only the authorized user can access the device. To set up biometric authentication, go to Settings > Security > Face & Fingerprint Unlock.

For users who store confidential work files or financial documents, enabling Secure Folder is highly recommended. This feature creates an encrypted space on your Pixel 9 Pro where sensitive files, apps, and images can be securely stored. To enable Secure Folder:

- Open Settings > Security > Secure Folder
- Follow the setup instructions and choose a PIN, pattern, or biometric authentication

Additionally, using encrypted cloud storage services, such as Google Drive with two-factor authentication (2FA), adds another layer of security for sensitive work documents and personal files.

For those who need to secure communications, using end-to-end encrypted messaging apps like Google Messages (RCS), Signal, or WhatsApp is recommended. These apps encrypt messages so that only the sender and recipient can read them, preventing hackers or third parties from intercepting private conversations.

Another security feature users should take advantage of is Find My Device, which helps locate, lock, or erase your Pixel 9 Pro remotely in case of theft or loss. To enable this feature:

- Go to Settings > Security > Find My Device
- Turn on Allow remote lock and erase

This feature allows you to track your phone in real time, lock it remotely, or wipe personal data if it falls into the wrong hands.

With the advanced security features and privacy tools available on the Pixel 9 Pro, users can confidently protect their personal data, secure their device against cyber threats, and browse the internet privately. By regularly updating the operating system, using VPNs, enabling Google Play Protect, and securing important files, the Pixel 9 Pro remains one of the most secure smartphones available. Taking advantage of these security measures ensures that your data stays protected, your device remains updated, and your personal information stays private at all times.

※ Elara Technova

Managing Storage and File Organization

Efficiently managing storage and organizing files on the Google Pixel 9 Pro is essential for keeping the device running smoothly, preventing unnecessary clutter, and ensuring easy access to important data. With the introduction of larger storage capacities and cloud integration, users can now store more files, photos, and apps than ever before. However, without proper management, storage can quickly become disorganized, leading to slower performance, reduced efficiency, and difficulty finding important files. This chapter will provide a comprehensive guide on using Google Files, expanding storage with cloud backup solutions, removing unnecessary files and apps, and exploring the best external storage options for users who need additional space.

Using Google Files for Better Storage Management

The Google Files app is the default file manager on the Pixel 9 Pro, designed to help users organize, clean, and manage files effectively. This app provides an intuitive interface for browsing files, freeing up storage, and quickly finding important documents, downloads, and media files.

One of the most useful features of Google Files is the Storage Cleaner, which automatically identifies junk files, duplicate content, and unused apps that may be taking up unnecessary space. To clear up storage space, follow these steps:

- Open Google Files on your Pixel 9 Pro.
- Tap on Clean at the bottom of the screen.

- Choose "Junk files" or "Duplicate files" and remove them to free up space.
- Review and delete large files, unused apps, and old downloads that are no longer needed.

Another useful feature is the "Search and Categorization" system, which automatically sorts files into categories such as Downloads, Documents, Audio, Videos, and Images. This makes it easier to locate specific files without manually searching through multiple folders.

Google Files also comes with an integrated file-sharing feature called Nearby Share, which allows users to send files wirelessly to other Android devices, Chromebooks, and Windows PCs without needing an internet connection. This is a fast and efficient way to transfer files, especially for those who need to share large media files or documents between devices.

For users who frequently download files and receive attachments, it's essential to periodically check and clear the Downloads folder to prevent storage from filling up with unnecessary files. Keeping downloads organized and deleting old or duplicate documents can significantly improve storage efficiency.

Cloud storage is one of the most effective ways to expand storage capacity without using physical external storage devices. Google Drive, Google Photos, and third-party cloud services offer a secure and accessible way to store files, photos, and documents without taking up space on the device.

Google Drive is the primary cloud storage service for Pixel users, offering 15GB of free storage, with options to purchase additional storage through Google One. Users can back up important files, work documents, and personal photos, ensuring that they remain accessible from any device, anywhere.

To set up Google Drive backup on the Pixel 9 Pro:

- Open Google Drive.
- Tap the Menu (three horizontal lines) and select Backups.
- Choose the type of content you want to back up (photos, videos, documents, or app data).
- Enable Auto-Backup to keep files continuously saved in the cloud.

For photo and video backups, Google Photos is the best option. It automatically syncs and stores media in the cloud, freeing up space on the device while ensuring easy access to photos and videos. To enable Google Photos backup:

- Open Google Photos.
- Tap Profile (top right corner) > Photos settings.
- Select Backup & sync and turn it on.
- Choose Storage quality settings to manage space effectively.

For users who require additional cloud storage, third-party options like Dropbox, Microsoft OneDrive, and Mega offer secure and scalable storage plans that integrate well with Android devices. These services allow users to sync files across multiple devices, share documents with others, and keep sensitive data safe from accidental loss.

Removing Unnecessary Files and Apps

Over time, devices accumulate unnecessary apps, cached data, and large files that take up valuable storage space. Regularly removing unused applications, duplicate files, and cache build-up helps keep the Pixel 9 Pro running efficiently and prevents sluggish performance.

To identify and uninstall unused apps, follow these steps:

- Open Settings > Apps.
- Tap See all apps to view the full list of installed applications.
- Look for apps that haven't been used in a long time.
- Select the app and tap Uninstall.

Another effective way to clear space is by managing cached data. Many apps store temporary files and cache that consume unnecessary storage. To clear cached data:

- Go to Settings > Storage.
- Tap Cached data and select Clear cache.

For users who install a lot of social media apps, messaging apps such as WhatsApp, Telegram, and Facebook Messenger tend to store large amounts of media files, voice notes, and chat backups. Clearing old messages, voice recordings, and media files can significantly free up storage space.

Additionally, using Lite versions of apps (such as Facebook Lite and Messenger Lite) can help reduce storage usage while still providing essential functionality.

For users who prefer physical storage expansion, external SSDs, USB-C flash drives, and OTG (On-The-Go) adapters offer additional storage capacity for media files, backups, and work documents.

The Pixel 9 Pro supports external storage via USB-C, allowing users to connect an external SSD or flash drive for seamless file transfers. To use an external storage device:

- Connect a USB-C flash drive or SSD to the Pixel 9 Pro using a USB-C OTG adapter.
- Open Google Files to access the external drive.
- Transfer files between the device and the external storage for backup or additional space.

Some of the best external storage devices for Pixel 9 Pro include:

- SanDisk Ultra Dual Drive USB-C – Ideal for quick file transfers between devices.
- Samsung T7 Portable SSD – Provides fast and secure external storage for large media files.

- Western Digital My Passport SSD – A reliable high-capacity option for work files and backups.

For photographers and videographers, external storage is essential for storing high-resolution photos, 4K videos, and large project files without filling up the device's internal storage.

Another useful feature is wireless external storage, such as the SanDisk iXpand Wireless Charger, which allows users to automatically back up files while charging their device.

Proper storage management and file organization play a crucial role in maintaining optimal performance and efficiency on the Pixel 9 Pro. By using Google Files for file management, expanding storage with cloud solutions, removing unnecessary apps and files, and utilizing external storage options, users can free up space, prevent slowdowns, and ensure important data is always accessible. Whether relying on cloud backups, external SSDs, or automatic cleanup tools, taking proactive steps in managing storage effectively enhances the overall usability and longevity of the Pixel 9 Pro.

Customizing Notifications and Alerts

The Google Pixel 9 Pro provides a wide range of notification customization options that allow users to control how alerts, messages, and updates appear on the device. Proper notification management is essential for minimizing distractions, improving focus, and ensuring important messages are never missed. With Android 15, users have access to advanced notification controls, adaptive sound settings, and focus modes, which help create a more personalized and efficient smartphone experience. This chapter explores the different ways to set up priority notifications, manage Do Not Disturb and Focus Modes, control app notifications, and utilize the Pixel's Adaptive Sound feature.

Setting Up Priority Notifications

Priority notifications allow users to filter out unnecessary alerts while ensuring that important messages, calls, and reminders come through without interruptions. This is especially useful for work environments, meetings, and personal time, where only essential notifications should be allowed.

To set up priority notifications on the Pixel 9 Pro, follow these steps:

1. Open Settings and navigate to Notifications.
2. Tap Conversations, where you can select important contacts whose messages will always be delivered, even when Do Not Disturb is enabled.
3. Under App Notifications, choose which apps are allowed to send urgent notifications.

4. Enable Priority Mode, which ensures selected notifications appear at the top of the list and bypass silent settings.

Another way to customize priority notifications is by using Notification Categories. Many apps offer customized alert levels, allowing users to set different types of notifications for messages, social media updates, promotions, and system alerts. By adjusting these categories, users can prevent unnecessary interruptions while staying informed about important updates.

For users who receive frequent calls and messages, the Starred Contacts feature ensures that calls and texts from selected contacts are always prioritized and not silenced, even when the device is in silent mode. This is useful for family members, emergency contacts, and essential work colleagues.

Managing Do Not Disturb and Focus Modes

The Do Not Disturb (DND) and Focus Modes on the Pixel 9 Pro are powerful tools for minimizing distractions and improving concentration. These features allow users to silence unwanted notifications, set custom schedules, and create exceptions for important alerts.

To enable and customize Do Not Disturb, follow these steps:

1. Open Settings > Sound & Vibration.
2. Tap Do Not Disturb and toggle it on.
3. Select Schedules to set automatic activation during specific hours, such as work hours, bedtime, or meetings.
4. Under Exceptions, choose which contacts, apps, or alarms are allowed to bypass DND.

For customized focus settings, users can enable Focus Mode, which temporarily disables distracting apps and notifications to help with productivity. To activate Focus Mode:

1. Open Settings > Digital Wellbeing & Parental Controls.
2. Tap Focus Mode and select apps to pause during the session.
3. Enable Scheduled Focus Mode to activate it automatically during work, study, or personal time.
4. Use the Quick Settings tile to enable or disable Focus Mode with a single tap.

Focus Mode also includes Take a Break options, allowing users to pause Focus Mode for short intervals before automatically resuming. This feature is particularly helpful for students, professionals, and anyone looking to minimize distractions while working.

Controlling App Notifications for Better Productivity

Managing app notifications effectively can reduce clutter, improve efficiency, and ensure important alerts are always noticed. The Pixel 9 Pro allows users to customize how notifications appear, modify sound and vibration settings, and group similar alerts for a more organized experience.

To adjust app notification settings:

1. Open Settings > Notifications.
2. Tap App Notifications and select an app to modify its alert preferences.
3. Choose between Silent, Default, or Priority notifications.
4. Use Notification Dots to show unread alerts without pop-up interruptions.
5. Enable Bubbles for supported messaging apps, allowing quick access to conversations without opening the full app.

For users who receive a large number of alerts, Notification Summary groups less important notifications into a scheduled digest, preventing frequent interruptions. This feature can be enabled in Settings > Notifications > Notification Summary.

Additionally, Lock Screen Notification Settings allow users to control what information appears on the lock screen. Users can choose to show full notifications, hide sensitive content, or completely disable lock screen alerts for privacy reasons.

For work-related apps such as Slack, Teams, and Google Calendar, setting custom sound and vibration patterns helps distinguish important work notifications from casual messages. Users can also enable Heads-Up Notifications for critical alerts that require immediate attention.

Using Google Pixel's Adaptive Sound Feature

The Adaptive Sound feature on the Google Pixel 9 Pro uses machine learning and real-time microphone adjustments to optimize audio levels based on the surrounding environment. This ensures that notification sounds, ringtones, and media playback remain clear and well-balanced in different situations.

To enable Adaptive Sound:

1. Open Settings > Sound & Vibration.
2. Tap Adaptive Sound and toggle it on.

3. The device will now automatically adjust volume and clarity based on background noise.

Adaptive Sound is especially beneficial for noisy environments, such as public transport, crowded areas, and workplaces. If a user is in a quiet room, the feature reduces volume to prevent unnecessary loudness. Conversely, in noisy surroundings, it boosts sound clarity to ensure notifications and ringtones remain audible.

In addition to Adaptive Sound, Custom Sound Profiles allow users to fine-tune audio settings for ringtones, notifications, and alarms. Users can set custom vibration patterns, assign unique ringtones for specific contacts, and adjust sound balance settings for an optimized listening experience.

Customizing notifications and alerts on the Pixel 9 Pro enhances productivity, minimizes distractions, and ensures that important messages and updates are always received on time. By setting up priority notifications, managing Do Not Disturb and Focus Modes, controlling app alerts, and enabling Adaptive Sound, users can create a more organized and personalized smartphone experience. Proper notification management allows users to stay focused during work, receive important alerts without unnecessary interruptions, and maintain control over their device's audio settings.

Selling and Upgrading Your Pixel

As technology advances, many users eventually decide to sell or upgrade their smartphones to keep up with the latest features, improved performance, and enhanced camera capabilities. If you own a Google Pixel 9 Pro and are considering selling or upgrading, it is essential to understand how to properly reset and wipe data, find the best platforms to trade in your device, compare the Pixel 9 Pro with other flagship phones, and choose the right upgrade option. This chapter provides detailed guidance on safely preparing your Pixel for resale or trade-in, exploring the best online marketplaces, understanding competitive comparisons, and selecting a new device that best suits your needs.

How to Reset and Wipe Data Safely

Before selling or trading in your Pixel 9 Pro, it is crucial to erase all personal data and reset the device to factory settings. This ensures that your private information, accounts, and stored files are completely removed, preventing unauthorized access.

To safely back up your data before resetting, follow these steps:

1. Open Settings > Google > Backup and ensure that all your data, including contacts, photos, apps, and settings, are backed up to your Google account.
2. Open Google Photos and verify that all your pictures and videos are synced to the cloud.
3. Use Google Drive or an external storage device to save important documents.

4. Sign out of all accounts, including Google, social media, and banking apps, to prevent unauthorized access after a reset.
5. Remove external storage, SIM cards, and eSIM profiles to avoid losing valuable data.

Once your data is backed up, perform a factory reset using these steps:

1. Open Settings > System > Reset Options.
2. Tap Erase All Data (Factory Reset).
3. Enter your device PIN or password when prompted.
4. Tap Erase All Data to confirm.

After the reset is complete, the phone will restart as a brand-new device, ready for its next owner. It is also advisable to manually sign out of your Google account from another device to ensure your Pixel is fully disassociated from your account.

Best Websites to Sell or Trade In Your Pixel

Once your Pixel 9 Pro has been reset, the next step is to find the best online marketplaces or trade-in programs that offer competitive pricing. Selling through trusted platforms ensures a safe transaction and the best value for your phone.

Top Platforms for Selling Your Pixel 9 Pro:

- Swappa – A reputable marketplace that allows users to sell their Pixel directly to buyers at competitive prices. Unlike trade-in programs, you can get higher payouts by setting your own price.
- eBay – Offers global exposure and the ability to auction your Pixel for the highest bid. Sellers should ensure they include clear photos and an honest description of the phone's condition.
- Facebook Marketplace & Craigslist – These platforms provide local selling opportunities where buyers can inspect the phone in person before purchasing. However, always meet in a safe location and avoid scams.
- Amazon Trade-In – Amazon offers store credit in exchange for your Pixel 9 Pro, which can be useful if you plan to upgrade through Amazon.
- Best Buy Trade-In – Best Buy provides an instant quote and offers gift cards that can be used towards a new purchase.
- Google Store Trade-In – Google offers an official trade-in program where users can exchange their old Pixel for a discount on a new Google device.

When selling privately, it is important to list your device with detailed information, including its condition, storage capacity, and included accessories. Providing high-quality photos and an accurate description increases buyer trust and helps secure a better price.

Before upgrading to a new smartphone, it is helpful to compare the Pixel 9 Pro with other flagship models to determine if an upgrade is necessary or if the current phone remains competitive.

Google Pixel 9 Pro vs. Pixel 8 Pro

- The Pixel 9 Pro features a faster Tensor G4 chip, offering better AI processing and improved efficiency.
- Camera enhancements in the Pixel 9 Pro include improved Night Sight, a larger sensor for better low-light performance, and advanced Magic Editor tools.
- The Pixel 9 Pro introduces Wi-Fi 7 support, allowing for faster internet speeds and lower latency.

Google Pixel 9 Pro vs. Samsung Galaxy S24 Ultra

- The Pixel 9 Pro focuses heavily on AI-powered photography, whereas the S24 Ultra offers 200MP camera capabilities with more manual controls for professionals.
- Samsung's One UI provides deeper customization, while the Pixel 9 Pro offers a cleaner Android experience with exclusive Google AI features.
- The S24 Ultra supports an S Pen for productivity, a feature not available on the Pixel.

Google Pixel 9 Pro vs. iPhone 15 Pro Max

- The iPhone 15 Pro Max is optimized for Apple's ecosystem, integrating seamlessly with Mac, iPad, and Apple Watch.
- The Pixel 9 Pro excels in computational photography, while Apple provides more consistent video recording quality.
- The iPhone 15 Pro Max features Apple's A17 Bionic chip, making it slightly faster for gaming and intensive tasks, but the Pixel 9 Pro offers AI-powered optimizations that enhance real-world performance.

Based on these comparisons, users must decide whether to stick with Google Pixel's AI-powered experience or explore other flagship models based on personal needs and budget.

Choosing the Best Upgrade Option

Upgrading to a new device depends on personal requirements, budget, and whether the current phone meets performance expectations. When selecting an upgrade, consider the following:

- Camera Performance – If photography is a priority, check newer Pixel models, Samsung's S-series, or iPhones that offer advanced camera hardware and software improvements.

- Battery Life and Charging – Newer devices often introduce improved battery efficiency and faster charging technologies, which may be beneficial for users who need longer-lasting power throughout the day.
- Software Updates and AI Features – If staying on the latest Android version with AI advancements is a priority, upgrading to Google's newest flagship ensures access to exclusive features.
- Storage and Connectivity – If higher storage capacity, better 5G performance, or Wi-Fi 7 support are required, a newer Pixel upgrade may be worth considering.

Users who enjoy the Pixel ecosystem but want better performance can upgrade to the next Google flagship, while those interested in exploring alternative features like stylus support or different camera setups might consider Samsung or Apple devices.

For those not ready for a full upgrade, considering a mid-cycle refresh by replacing the battery, optimizing storage, or updating accessories can extend the Pixel 9 Pro's usability for another year or more.

Selling or upgrading the Pixel 9 Pro requires careful data backup, a secure factory reset, and choosing the right resale or trade-in platform. Understanding how the Pixel 9 Pro compares to other flagship devices helps users decide whether an upgrade is necessary or if their current device remains competitive. Selecting the right upgrade option depends on factors like photography needs, battery life improvements, and software features. Whether selling, trading in, or upgrading, making an informed decision ensures the best value and experience moving forward.

Maximizing Resale Value

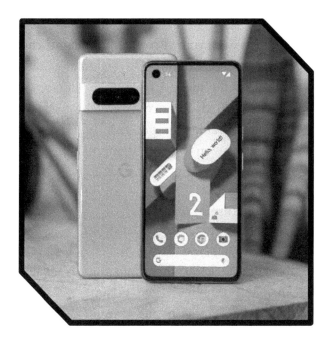

Smartphone technology advances rapidly, and many users choose to sell or trade in their devices when upgrading. If you own a Google Pixel 9 Pro and plan to sell or trade it in, maximizing its resale value is essential. A well-maintained phone will fetch a higher price, attract more buyers, and provide a smoother transaction experience. This chapter explores how to keep your device in excellent condition, where to find the best selling platforms, how to use Google's official trade-in program, and the crucial steps to take before finalizing the sale.

Keeping Your Device in Excellent Condition

The condition of your Pixel 9 Pro significantly affects its resale value. Buyers and trade-in programs offer the highest payouts for devices that are well-maintained, free from scratches, dents, or display issues. Taking proper care of your phone ensures it remains in top condition, making it more appealing to potential buyers.

Protecting the Display and Body

Using a high-quality screen protector helps prevent scratches, cracks, and fingerprint smudges, ensuring the display remains in pristine condition. Additionally, a durable phone case protects against drops, dents, and scratches. A well-protected phone not only lasts longer but also retains its original appearance, increasing its resale value.

Maintaining Battery Health

A healthy battery is a major selling point, as buyers prefer phones that hold a charge efficiently. To keep the battery in optimal condition:

- Avoid letting the battery drain completely before recharging.
- Use the original charger or a certified replacement to prevent battery degradation.
- Enable Adaptive Battery under settings to optimize power consumption.
- Reduce exposure to extreme heat or cold, which can shorten battery lifespan.

Cleaning and Presentation

Before listing your Pixel 9 Pro for sale, ensure it is clean and free from dust, dirt, or fingerprints. Use a soft microfiber cloth and a mild cleaning solution to wipe down the screen and body. Keeping the charging port, speakers, and buttons free from debris ensures smooth functionality, making the phone more desirable to buyers.

Finding the Best Buyer Platforms

Once your phone is in top condition, the next step is finding the right platform to sell it. Several online and offline options exist, each offering different price points, selling conditions, and levels of convenience.

Online Marketplaces

- Swappa – One of the best platforms for selling used smartphones, Swappa connects sellers directly with buyers. It has low seller fees and allows users to set their price, typically yielding a higher return compared to trade-in programs.

- eBay – Offers the ability to auction your Pixel 9 Pro or set a fixed price. eBay attracts a large audience, increasing your chances of getting a competitive price, but sellers must be aware of listing fees and buyer protection policies.
- Facebook Marketplace & Craigslist – These platforms enable local selling, eliminating the need for shipping fees. However, it is crucial to meet buyers in safe, public locations and verify payment before handing over the device.

Trade-In Programs

For those who prefer hassle-free transactions, trade-in programs offer an easy way to exchange the Pixel 9 Pro for credit or cash. However, trade-in values tend to be lower than private sales.

Understanding Google's Trade-In Program

Google offers an official trade-in program, allowing users to exchange their old devices for a discount on a new Google product. This is an attractive option for those upgrading within the Google ecosystem.

How the Google Trade-In Program Works

1. Visit the Google Store – Navigate to Google's official trade-in page and enter details about your device, including its model, condition, and storage capacity.
2. Get an Instant Quote – Google provides an estimated trade-in value based on your phone's condition. This value is subject to inspection once the device is received.
3. Send in Your Device – After confirming your trade-in, Google will send a prepaid shipping label. Pack the device securely to avoid damage during transit.
4. Receive Credit – Once Google inspects the phone and confirms its condition, the trade-in value is applied as credit toward a new purchase or issued as a Google Store credit.

While convenient, the Google trade-in program typically offers lower payouts than selling through private marketplaces. However, it is ideal for users who want a simple, straightforward trade-in experience without dealing with direct buyers.

What to Do Before Selling Your Pixel

Before selling or trading in your Pixel 9 Pro, taking the right precautions ensures a secure and smooth transition.

Backup Important Data

Before resetting your phone, it is essential to back up all important files, contacts, messages, and photos. Use Google One or Google Drive to store backups in the cloud. To back up your data:

1. Go to Settings > Google > Backup.
2. Enable Google One Backup for photos, contacts, and app data.
3. Use Google Photos to sync all images and videos.

Sign Out of Accounts

To prevent the next owner from accessing your information, log out of all accounts, including:

- Google Account – Navigate to Settings > Accounts > Google and remove your account.
- Social Media and Banking Apps – Sign out of all logged-in services.
- Find My Device – Disable Find My Device under Settings > Security to unlink the phone from your account.

Perform a Factory Reset

Resetting your Pixel 9 Pro ensures all personal data, passwords, and saved files are erased. To perform a factory reset:

1. Go to Settings > System > Reset Options.

2. Select Erase All Data (Factory Reset).
3. Confirm the reset and wait for the phone to restart as a brand-new device.

Include Accessories for a Better Deal

If possible, selling your Pixel 9 Pro with its original box, charger, and accessories can increase its resale value. Buyers are often willing to pay more for a device with a charger, case, and additional accessories.

Maximizing the resale value of your Google Pixel 9 Pro requires proper maintenance, finding the right selling platform, and preparing the device correctly before the sale. Keeping the phone in excellent condition, selling through reliable marketplaces, and backing up and resetting data securely ensures a smooth transition and a higher return. Whether choosing a private sale, trade-in program, or online marketplace, following these steps will help get the best possible price for your Pixel 9 Pro while ensuring the new owner receives a clean, functional device.

Future-Proofing Your Google Pixel 9 Pro

Technology evolves at a rapid pace, and smartphones become outdated faster than ever. However, the Google Pixel 9 Pro is designed to remain relevant for years with continuous software updates, AI enhancements, and cutting-edge hardware. Future-proofing your Pixel 9

Pro ensures that you continue to get the best performance, latest features, and highest security protections for as long as possible. This chapter explores how to prepare for Android 16 and beyond, maximize longevity with software tweaks, anticipate new AI-powered features, and understand the future direction of the Pixel lineup.

Preparing for Android 16 and Future Updates

One of the biggest advantages of owning a Google Pixel device is access to timely Android updates. Google provides at least five years of software and security updates, meaning your Pixel 9 Pro will continue to receive new features and improvements long after its release. Staying on top of system updates is crucial for enhancing performance, fixing bugs, and ensuring compatibility with new apps and services.

How to Keep Your Pixel Updated

To ensure your Pixel 9 Pro is always running the latest version of Android:

1. Enable Automatic Updates – Go to Settings > System > Software Update and toggle on Auto Update. This ensures your device downloads and installs the latest Android version as soon as it is available.

2. Check for Updates Manually – If you prefer to update at your convenience, go to Settings > System > Software Update > Check for Updates to see if a new version is available.
3. Join the Android Beta Program – If you want early access to upcoming features, consider enrolling in Google's Android Beta Program. However, beta software can sometimes have bugs, so it is recommended for advanced users only.

Google also rolls out security patches and minor updates every month, fixing vulnerabilities and improving system stability. Keeping your Pixel 9 Pro updated ensures it remains fast, secure, and compatible with future apps and services.

Maximizing Longevity with Software Tweaks

Even with top-tier hardware, a phone's longevity depends on how well it is maintained. By optimizing your Pixel 9 Pro's settings, managing resources wisely, and adopting good usage habits, you can extend its lifespan and ensure peak performance for years.

Optimizing Performance Settings

- Limit Background Processes – Too many background apps consume memory and slow down your phone. Go to Developer Options >

Background Process Limit and reduce the number of apps running in the background.

- Disable Unnecessary Animations – Reducing animation speeds can make the device feel faster and more responsive. Adjust this under Developer Options > Window Animation Scale and set it to 0.5x.
- Use Lite Versions of Apps – Apps like Google Go, YouTube Go, and Facebook Lite consume fewer resources and battery, ensuring smoother operation over time.

Maintaining Battery Health for Long-Term Use

Battery degradation is one of the main reasons smartphones lose performance over time. To keep your Pixel 9 Pro's battery in excellent condition:

- Avoid full discharges – Charge your phone before it drops below 20%, and unplug it before reaching 100% to extend battery longevity.
- Use Adaptive Charging – This feature slows down charging overnight to preserve battery health. Enable it under Settings > Battery > Adaptive Charging.
- Minimize Fast Charging – While convenient, excessive fast charging generates heat, which can wear out the battery over time. Use a regular charger when possible for longer battery life.

By following these maintenance steps, your Pixel 9 Pro can maintain strong battery health, fast performance, and long-term usability, ensuring it remains a powerful device for years.

Upcoming AI Features and Enhancements

Google continues to push the boundaries of artificial intelligence (AI) and machine learning (ML), making the Pixel 9 Pro one of the smartest smartphones available. Future updates will introduce even more AI-powered capabilities to enhance productivity, photography, and user experience.

Potential AI-Powered Enhancements for Google Pixel

- More Advanced Call Screening – Google Assistant already filters spam calls, but future updates may improve real-time call transcription and context-aware responses.
- Smarter Google Lens Integration – Expect better AI-driven object recognition, shopping recommendations, and real-time text translation.
- Enhanced AI Photography – Google is likely to introduce even better automatic photo editing tools, allowing users to remove distractions, enhance colors, and adjust lighting instantly.
- AI-Powered Battery Optimization – Google is working on algorithms that dynamically adjust power usage based on your daily habits,

ensuring longer battery life without manual adjustments.

As Google refines its AI technology, Pixel users will benefit from increasingly intuitive and automated features, making everyday tasks easier and more efficient.

The Future of Google's Pixel Lineup

Google's Pixel series continues to evolve, introducing cutting-edge hardware, AI capabilities, and deeper Android integration with each new release. If you're thinking about future upgrades, understanding the direction of Google's Pixel lineup can help you decide when and how to make your next move.

What to Expect from Future Pixel Devices

- More Powerful Tensor Chips – Google is continuously improving its Tensor chip technology, bringing better AI processing, faster speeds, and improved security.
- Foldable and Expandable Display Options – Rumors suggest that Google may introduce a foldable Pixel phone, expanding its lineup to compete with Samsung's Galaxy Fold series.
- Extended Software Support – Google is moving toward longer software support for Pixel

devices, possibly increasing security updates to seven years or more.

- New AI-Based Features – Future Pixel devices may feature advanced AI assistants, real-time voice translation, and even AI-generated wallpapers.

Owning a Pixel 9 Pro puts you at the forefront of Google's innovation, ensuring access to new AI tools, camera technology, and software improvements for years to come.

The Google Pixel 9 Pro is built to last, offering regular software updates, advanced AI capabilities, and a robust hardware design. By staying updated with Android releases, optimizing performance settings, and maintaining good battery habits, you can ensure your device remains fast, efficient, and secure for years. Google's commitment to artificial intelligence, security enhancements, and user experience refinements makes the Pixel series an exciting and future-proof investment. Whether you plan to keep your device long-term or upgrade in the future, following these best practices will help you get the most out of your Pixel 9 Pro, ensuring a seamless and powerful smartphone experience.

※ Elara Technova